HIGH
PERFORMANCE

HIGH
PERFORMANCE
Lessons from the Best on Becoming Your Best

Jake Humphrey
Prof Damian Hughes

1 3 5 7 9 10 8 6 4 2

Random House Business
20 Vauxhall Bridge Road
London SW1V 2SA

Random House Business is part of the Penguin Random House
group of companies whose addresses can be found at
global.penguinrandomhouse.com.

First published by Random House Business in 2021

www.penguin.co.uk

A CIP catalogue record for this book is available from the British Library.

ISBN 9781847943682 (Hardback)
ISBN 9781847943699 (Trade Paperback)

Typeset in 11.25/16.7 pt Sabon LT W1G
by Integra Software Services Pvt. Ltd, Pondicherry

Printed and bound in Great Britain by Clays Ltd, Elcograf S.p.A.

The authorised representative in the EEA is Penguin Random House Ireland,
Morrison Chambers, 32 Nassau Street, Dublin D02 YH68

Penguin Random House is committed to a sustainable future for
our business, our readers and our planet. This book is made from
Forest Stewardship Council® certified paper.

CONTENTS

High performance is a habit like any other. With time, it becomes as natural as brushing your teeth.

NOTHING IS FIXED

Jake

Failure changed my life.

It was the mid-1990s. I had just finished my A-Levels, and I had my life mapped out. Nobody thought I was on track for greatness, least of all myself. I had been the epitome of average at my school in Norwich: I wasn't on any sports teams, I wasn't part of any societies or clubs, I couldn't act or sing. In fact, I was so average I'd been fired from McDonald's a few months previously for a 'lack of communication skills'.

Life wasn't awful, but it wasn't amazing either. And so my horizons were pretty narrow. I had a place lined up at the University of Nottingham to study media; after that, I was planning to get a job back in my hometown, maybe for the local newspaper. It was a vague plan – the details of how exactly I was going to get that job were pretty woolly. But somehow it felt like my destiny. I never dreamed of a career that would take me much further than Norwich, let alone around the world.

After a summer of drinking in East Anglia and holidaying in Faliraki, it was finally A-Level results day. I clambered into my mum's pistachio green VW Polo and drove to collect my results, with my younger brother in tow. Upon arriving at the 1950s complex that housed my run-down state school, I made my way to the table for students whose surnames started with 'H'. As I was passed the envelope, I prepared myself for what was on the page, fully expecting grades good enough to get my university place.

I needed B, C, C.

I got E, N, U.

I didn't even know what an 'N' was. I was told by a teacher that it stands for 'narrow'. As in, I had narrowly missed getting an E. But I'd failed anyway.

A total disaster.

Or so I thought.

Today, I believe those awful grades were the single best thing that ever happened to me.

Weeks later, having processed my failure – and apologised to my parents a few thousand times – I was back at the same school studying for my retakes. During my first week back, my politics teacher, Mr Brogan, read out a letter that had been sent to our politics class. It invited students to appear on a new cable channel, Rapture TV, to talk about political issues.

Despite my massive exam humiliation, I was young, naive and inexplicably certain I would make an excellent pundit. I jumped at the opportunity to work in TV. The next week, I rocked up at Rapture's office wearing the late nineties staple of a Sweater Shop top and baggy jeans. I told them about the fast-food sacking and the A-Level catastrophe, and asked them if I could give the channel a hand. I promised to do anything and everything: not just opining on politics, but also making tea, operating the phones – whatever they needed. They agreed – they needed all the help they could get – and I started working at Rapture for £5 cash each weekend.

Two decades on, it's tempting to think this moment was part of my destiny – the first step in some inevitable path into my life in television. It wasn't. In the wake of my A-Level cock-up, I had no real life plan, let alone any understanding of how TV worked. My cash-in-hand job wasn't the result of some grand strategy. It was luck.

But it turned out to be the start of something great. Even though Rapture would go bust a few years later, I remember my days there fondly. It was my first time in a TV studio, and I loved it – the bustle of the production crew, the excitement of going on air. More importantly, the experience caused me to reconsider my approach to success. You see, my A-Level disaster – and my Rapture TV recovery – was the first time I started to think about what it meant to achieve your potential.

Until then, I'd thought that success in life was simple: you either had talent or you didn't. If you did, life would be easy; if you didn't, life would be hard. This principle led some people to lives of unimaginable success, and others to lives of mundanity. That's why, until that point, I'd had so little ambition. If I wasn't naturally talented, there wasn't much I could do about it.

My job at Rapture made me see things differently. I had failed my A-Levels, but I'd got back up on my feet. By failing, I'd discovered new possibilities. If the biggest failure in my entire life had led to this exciting opportunity, what else could failure teach me?

That experience marked the beginning of my journey to writing this book. As my career progressed – from Rapture TV to the BBC and now BT Sport – I found myself surrounded by people who had realised their dreams. I reported from F1 pit lanes, Olympic stadiums and Champions League finals. I had lunch with Lewis Hamilton, shared a TV screen with Michael Johnson, even went to a reception at 10 Downing Street. Every day, I was lucky enough to spend time with world-beating athletes, entrepreneurs and creatives.

The old me would have thought that these people were just born high achievers, that they had something that I didn't. But the more time I spent with them, the more wrong I realised I was.

Sure, many of these individuals had natural skill. But that wasn't how they had achieved success. There are tonnes of people with talent, and not all of them make it. In time, I realised the high achievers I met had triumphed thanks to their own persistence. They had kept their motivation up through dozens of setbacks. They had worked hard to develop a winner's mindset and a winner's habits. They had surrounded themselves with people who encouraged them to be their best. In short, they had *turned* themselves into high performers.

It was the same lesson I had learned after my A-Level fiasco. To unlock your potential, you don't need to be a born leader. You just need to be ready to try, fail, and try again.

Over the past twenty years, this insight has changed my life. It's what led me to take some of the biggest risks of my career – whether that was auditioning for a job at the BBC in 2001, founding a production company, Whisper, in 2010 with my wife and a friend, or upending my career to join the upstart BT Sport in 2013.

Along the way, I had my share of failures, some humiliating. But, in the end, I managed to achieve more than I once thought possible – winning awards for my presenting, fronting some of the world's biggest sporting events and turning Whisper into a company with hundreds of staff and a turnover in the tens of millions.

I had uncovered the greatest secret of high performance. The teenage me had been wrong. Nothing is fixed. And you can change almost anything about 'you' if you want to.

It's this principle that led me to create the *High Performance* podcast – and, ultimately, to write this book. In the late 2010s, I realised I was entering my third decade as a television presenter. I had learned so much from the high performers I'd met. They hadn't just taught me that we can all change our lives – they'd shown me how to do so. I realised it was high time to share what they had taught me with the world. My team and I decided to create a podcast that examined the outlook of the world's highest-achieving people and what we could all learn from them.

A nice idea. But a complicated one to execute. We soon realised that getting the most out of our interviewees wouldn't just mean hearing their stories – it would involve digging deep into their psychology and behaviour. Soon I realised I needed someone to help me understand the science behind high performance. After all, I was the kid who got E, N, U at A-Level.

The podcast didn't just need a presenter. It also needed a professor.

And that's where Damian Hughes came in.

Damian

Being raised by a boxing coach has its ups and downs. On the one hand, you learn valuable skills like how to skip rope, throw a punch and cope under pressure. On the other, you learn to exercise extreme caution when answering back.

My upbringing was very different to Jake's. While he was growing up in a small village near Norwich, I spent my adolescence in inner-city Manchester. In a boxing gym, to be precise. Or, as the *Telegraph* once described it, in 'an unrelenting place', in which 'only the foolhardy would park a car … unless they enjoyed returning to find their vehicle propped up on small piles of bricks, its wheels expertly removed by a team who works quicker than Michael Schumacher's pit crew.'[1] Charming.

The *Telegraph* had ventured to Collyhurst all those years ago to meet my father, the boxing coach Brian Hughes. In his gym, world-class standards were expected. Many of his protégés went on to achieve success in the Olympics and World Championships. In 2017, my dad even had a street named in his honour to mark the difference he had made to so many people's lives, inside and outside the ring.

From a young age, I realised what made my dad unique: he had a knack for getting people to be all they could be. Sometimes he was affectionate, sometimes he was tough – but he was consistent in wanting everyone to live up to their potential, both as athletes and as people.

One moment stands out in particular. I remember being thirteen, and sparring against an opponent who was inexperienced and nervous. Naturally, I thought the appropriate response was to embarrass him as much as possible. I was acting like a dick.

As I was climbing out of the ring, feeling pretty pleased with myself, my dad intervened and asked me to carry on training for a little longer. He signalled to a vastly more experienced boxer to step into the ring with me. Unsurprisingly, my new opponent spent the entire time evading my blows – and making sure that everyone in the gym saw that I couldn't land a punch. All my peers were watching me eat a slice of humble pie.

When I got out of the ring, I was red-faced – and not just from the exercise. 'How do you feel?' my Dad enquired. I stood there sullenly. 'You are feeling the same way you made your first opponent feel,' he said. 'Never, ever bully anyone again.'

It was a tough lesson. But thirty years later, I feel that it was formative. If I am ever tempted to behave in an unpleasant way, I remember what my dad taught me that day: that kindness, decency and humility are always a far better option. My dad had got me to be the best person I could be.

During those teenage years in his gym, I often found myself wondering how – despite having no formal training, and owning no more than a humble, sweat-soaked room in Manchester – my dad had learned methods like these. He seemed to intuitively know how to get people to live up to their potential, whether by becoming world-class boxers or just better people.

These experiences sparked a lifelong interest in the secrets of high performance. You might call it 'me-search', inspired by those early personal experiences in Collyhurst. After leaving home, I became one of the first people in my family to attend university – and set out to find some of the answers.

Three decades later, and I've made it my life's work – as a writer, consultant and coach – to understand high-performing cultures: environments where people perform to their full potential, just like my dad's gym. It's been a wonderful, fascinating and eclectic ride. Over the years, I've worked alongside the managers of world-class sports teams as they are lauded, examined, challenged and ridiculed by fans. I've served on the coaching teams of three separate world cup tournaments in three different sports. I have stood in the corner of a number of world title fights. I even once had my work praised by the late Muhammad Ali, which was just as surreal and humbling as you'd imagine.

Along the way, I've tried to make sense of what makes high-achieving people tick – not just in sport, but also in business and in life. Over the years, I've consulted for companies ranging from Unilever to Sky, Santander to Mars, on how to create a culture of excellence. And, in 2010, I was appointed as an honorary professor of organisational psychology and change at Manchester Metropolitan University.

So, when Jake approached me to help present the *High Performance* podcast, it felt like the logical next step. On a balmy summer's day in Norwich, the two of us met up for a coffee and a chat. We soon realised that we each brought something to the table.

Jake was the interviewer, with a knack for getting high achievers to open up about their experiences. I was the prof, who understood the psychology of high-performing people.

High Performance was born.

BOXERS, BALLET DANCERS, BILLIONAIRES

When we first launched the *High Performance* podcast, the goal was simple. We wanted to speak to the world's greatest sportspeople, coaches and entrepreneurs about how they got to where they are. And we wanted anyone who listened to have the chance to learn from them.

We're well on our way to meeting that goal. In the podcast's first eighteen months, we spoke to former Liverpool captain Steven Gerrard, film star Matthew McConaughey, Gold-winning Olympian Kelly Holmes, South African rugby skipper Siya Kolisi, entrepreneur Holly Tucker, renowned ballet dancer Marcelino Sambé, Manchester United manager Ole Gunnar Solskjær, and many more.

Some of the revelations have been extraordinary. Jonny Wilkinson described how he now regards washing the dishes in much the same way as he regards scoring the winning points in the 2003 Rugby World Cup final. Others have been moving. The entrepreneur Jo Malone recounted the lessons she learned during her battle with cancer, explaining how illness had given her a new take on leading a team. And the podcast has taken us across the country, from meeting Chris Hoy in a storm-battered studio in Manchester's Northern Quarter to hosting workshops on high performance at the top of the BT Tower in London.

We knew we were on to something brilliant from the moment we sat down with our first interviewee, Rio Ferdinand (football pundit, former Manchester United defender and, as he told us, one-time avid ballet dancer). But still the scale of the response surprised us. Launching in March, 2020, into a world in the grips of the coronavirus pandemic, *High Performance* connected with people. Soon, people were reaching out to tell us that our series had changed their outlook and their life. We've received messages from international CEOs, small-business owners, teachers and sporting leaders. Our personal highlight came in the run-up to the UEFA European Football Championship in 2021: England manager Gareth Southgate appeared on the podcast and thanked us for 'helping get me through lockdown'.

But with time we came to realise that there are some things a podcast can't do. When you're focused on the story of any one individual, it's easy to lose sight of the bigger picture. Each episode offered one fascinating lesson, maybe two. But we had our sights on something more holistic. In this book, we have brought together the insights of dozens of interviewees to offer a one-stop guide to achieving high performance.

That might sound optimistic. After all, our interviewees are an eclectic bunch – not many podcasts feature boxers, ballet dancers and billionaires from one week to the next. Could such a diverse array of people really have much in common? It's true that each interviewee had their own idiosyncrasies. Who but the world-beating sprinter Dina Asher-Smith could simultaneously charm us and grinningly recount how, if you crossed into her lane, she would 'run right through you'? Who but the entrepreneur Holly Tucker could tell us about how success made her stop being the 'Holly Hurricane' (and what she did about it)? Who but the film star Matthew McConaughey could explain how to transform from a run-of-the-mill 'rom com guy' to an Oscar-winning dramatic actor?

Yet as the podcast grew, we realised that all our high performers shared certain characteristics. Whether they had achieved excellence in sport or business, film or music, they emphasised the importance of taking responsibility for their actions. They talked about the need to turn one-off behaviours into consistent habits. And they discussed the need to create a culture of high performance that went beyond any one individual and spread into their wider team.

Whether they realised it or not, our guests were sketching out a roadmap to high performance. From mindset to daily habits, leadership to team culture, our high performers were pointing the way to excellence for us all.

THREE STEPS TO HIGH PERFORMANCE

Even armed with a roadmap, the path to high performance can be daunting. When we met the multimillionaire businessman Steve Morgan, he told us his golden rule for achieving excellence: 'Thou shalt work like hell.' Many of our guests shared his sentiment.

For that reason, we have tried to make this book as simple and straightforward as possible, so that you can dedicate all your efforts to your high performance journey. It is divided into three sections, each exploring a discrete element of achieving excellence. In each section, we've included a handful of chapters – or 'lessons' – on how you can become the best 'you' possible.

In Section I, we'll introduce the high performance mindset. Before we can act like high performers, we need to think like high performers. As Kelly Holmes told us, the majority of success is in the mind: it's 'only 20 per cent talent', as she put it. And, as we'll see in these opening chapters, high performers view the world in a strikingly different way from the rest of us. We'll learn how high performers take responsibility for every one of their actions; how they manage to keep motivated; and how they keep their emotions under control under extreme pressure.

 'Success is only 20 per cent talent.'

Kelly Holmes

With the psychological foundations of high performance in place, we move on to Section II – about high performance behaviour. High performance isn't just about how you think; it's about how you act. Here, we'll examine the peculiar and remarkable things high performers do. We'll describe how high performers identify and play to their strengths, how they solve problems in a creative and surprising manner, and how they turn odd moments of high performance into consistent, deeply ingrained behaviours. High performance is a habit like any other. With time, it becomes as natural as brushing your teeth.

But nobody wants to be a high performer alone. In fact, nobody can be a high performer alone: as we'll learn in Section III, the most consistently high-performing people operate as part of brilliant teams. And so, in this section, our focus is on how we as individuals can each help create a high-performing group. There are two key factors. First, we can harness the power of leadership – giving clear direction to our peers on what to do. Second, through culture-building, we can create an atmosphere in which everyone feels safe, at home and able to perform at their best. Best of all, we'll show that one need not be a CEO or team captain to help build a high-performing culture – you just need to be part of a team and prepared to take charge.

Think of these three areas as concentric circles, each fitting neatly inside the next. The order is deliberate. High performance begins in the mind: before you can behave like a high achiever, you must think like one. Next comes behaviour, in which you turn that newfound psychological state into concrete actions. Then, through that behaviour, you can pass a culture of high performance on to your wider team, which will help both you and them. High performance ripples outwards from our minds, to our actions, to our teams.

But we're also aware that, in the bustle of our busy lives, it's not always easy to carve out three (or six, or ten) hours to read a book cover to cover. And so, throughout the book, we've scattered information boxes that will help you apply our high

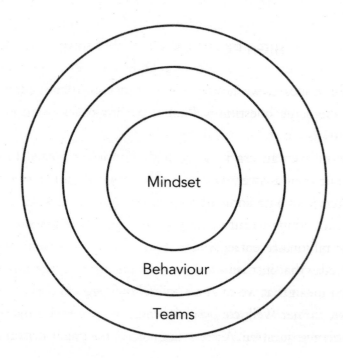

performers' insights right away. In some cases, these boxes offer practical exercises that will challenge you and make you think. In others, they describe key moments from our own high performance journeys.

We call these boxes 'high performance pit stops'. The name comes from the fastest sport in the world – Formula 1. We think high performance is a lot like an F1 race. The most high-achieving people operate like a well-run F1 operation, with every component – from the wheels, to the engine, to the chassis – coming together to drive the car forward. And in F1, races are often won by those who manage their time in the pit stop most effectively.

In this book too, the pit stops should make all the difference. They will challenge you to think about how to use the *High Performance* lessons in your own life, and give you the confidence to apply them.

HIGH PERFORMANCE FOR YOU

On the podcast, we have taken to opening all our interviews with the same question: 'What does high performance mean to you?'

Before we can crack on with this book, you need to work out your own answer. You see, while *High Performance* draws on interviews with some of the world's most remarkable people, we're not trying to turn everyone into an Olympic gold medallist or billionaire entrepreneur. For many of us – your authors included – that just isn't feasible (not for now, at least). But this doesn't mean that we can't all be high performers.

How come? Well, consider the sheer variety of the answers to our opening question. According to one of the greatest footballers of the twenty-first century, Steven Gerrard, high performance means going 'all in' with whatever task you are facing. According to Kelly Jones, lead singer of the rock band Stereophonics, high performance means discipline: doing the right thing every time, even when nobody is watching. The shortest definition came from England Rugby head coach Eddie Jones, who gave us a three-word summary: 'Embrace the grind.' Between them, our interviewees have amassed hundreds of Commonwealth and Olympic titles, set world records and built and sold businesses worth billions – yet no two high performers can agree on a definition.

Clearly high performance varies from individual to individual. It means something different to a professional footballer trying to win the Champions League and someone taking part in a Saturday tournament. You need to work out what high performance means in your life.

But how? The question stumped your authors for the first five months of making the podcast. By the time we reached the second series, we had heard over thirty different definitions of high performance but were little closer to getting an answer. Until, that was, we met the football manager Phil Neville.

Neville's career had been characterised by a willingness to accept hard challenges. He had left his boyhood team, Manchester United, to become captain at Everton, where he ended his playing career. After retiring from professional football, he was named manager of England Women. He helped the Lionesses win their second ever SheBelieves Cup, get through to the semi-finals in the World Cup and qualify for the Tokyo Olympics. Here was someone who knew about high performance – and we had a hunch his insights wouldn't disappoint.

Sure enough, they didn't. While we were chatting over a cup of tea in the hotel he co-owns opposite Old Trafford, Neville casually shared the mantra he had adopted during his playing career: 'Do the best you can, where you are, with what you have got.'

 'Do the best you can, where you are, with what you have got.' Phil Neville

The simplicity of those thirteen words struck a chord. Even though the precise definition of high performance differs from person to person, Neville's phrase summarises what all high performers have in common.

In this rendering, high performance isn't about the external trappings of success. Neville didn't mention any of the trinkets he had gained during his career – the trophies, the overflowing bank accounts, the mansion. Instead, he emphasised being a high performer in the moment.

Do the best you can. Where you are. With what you've got. If you're a teacher, that might mean spending extra time listening to a student who seems bored and disengaged from school life. If you work in business, it might involve investing extra time in polishing that important sales pitch. If the most important thing in your life is family, high performance might be as simple as spending quality time with the ones you love. We can't tell everyone who reads this book where this definition will take them. But before turning to Lesson 1, take a moment to ponder what it means for you. Choose an area of your life – your relationship, your career, your interests – and imagine what doing the best you can with what you've got would look like.

You can be a high performer at your desk in an office, or on the pitch in your Saturday league. You can be a high performer whether you're just starting your first job or are a retiree embarking on a new hobby. As Neville put it, 'You can be born with unbelievable ability, you can be born with not much ability.'

Wherever you are, whoever you are, high performance is within your reach. We hope this book will help grasp it.

High Performance Mindset

When we go through hell, it's human to look for someone to blame. But blame is useless. All that matters is how we respond.

TAKE RESPONSIBILITY

'I think that's life. What happened to me is how life works – you have obstacles that are thrown in your way.'

From his relaxed tone, Billy Monger could easily have been telling us about a small setback – losing a game of football, or missing out on a job at interview. Little about his demeanour let on that he was describing losing his legs in a catastrophic racing crash.

'Obviously mine is recognised because it was quite a big accident, and a lot of people know about it,' he told us. 'But in terms of your mindset and how you get over something like that – I don't see my accident as too different.'

Few people who witnessed the crash would have described it in such understated terms. In 2017, Monger been participating in a British F4 championship race at Donington Park. The seventeen-year-old had been battling through the pack when he came across a slowing car. A train of cars between them had obscured Monger's vision, leaving him unable to brake quickly enough to avoid colliding with the vehicle in front, causing Monger to spin off the track.

At first, Billy thought he was OK. When the paramedics arrived, he told them to attend to the other driver. In fact, the adrenaline was preventing him from feeling his injuries. It took ninety minutes to cut Billy free from the car and load him into an air ambulance. 'The whole family was there,' his father, Robert, would later explain to the media. 'We were in the pit lane. They shut the big screens down straight away but I knew it was quite bad with the amount of medical cars going out of the pit lane.'[1]

Monger was placed into an induced coma and would remain hospitalised for the next five weeks. When he woke up he discovered that both of his legs had been amputated – one just above the knee, the other just below.

Yet when we met Monger, three years after his crash, he was optimistic. 'Obviously there are moments where something will frustrate me,' he told us. 'Often it's the small things that get on your nerves – little things you can't do.' In general, though, his outlook is optimistic: 'I'm quite a happy, chilled-out person. I don't normally let things get to me … I was as happy before as I am now.'

And how does he think about the crash today? It's simple, he said. 'I knew it wasn't my fault but how I reacted was my responsibility.'

'I knew it wasn't my fault but how
I reacted was my responsibility.'
Billy Monger

Monger placed careful emphasis on two words: *fault* and *responsibility*. It was a powerful insight. Nobody could have suggested that the crash was Monger's fault – it was a result of catastrophic bad luck. And nobody would have blamed him if the double amputation had sent him into a downward spiral.

But it hadn't. Monger had realised that, even when things happen to us that aren't our fault, there is one thing we can control: our reactions. This is what he meant by 'responsibility' – taking control of your reaction to the things life throws at you. As we'll learn in this chapter, the ability to distinguish between 'fault' and 'responsibility' is one of the key skills – perhaps *the* key skill – in a high performer's mental toolkit.

In Monger's case, taking responsibility for his response meant working hard to get his old life back. 'People like to ask questions about my accident and how I've changed, but in my head I'm still the same person as I was,' he said. And so he wouldn't let the accident stand in the way of his passion for racing. Within eleven weeks of his accident, Monger was back at the wheel. 'I still had forty pins in my leg,' he laughed. Today, Monger drives in an adapted car – and still harbours ambitions to become an F1 champion.

Monger's experience offers a masterclass in overcoming adversity. When we go through hell, it's human to look for someone to blame. But blame is useless. All that matters is how we respond.

This concept is often misunderstood. Taking responsibility isn't about taking it in the neck for things that aren't your fault. Nor is it about forcing a smile on to your face when the entire world is crumbling around you. A person who takes responsibility can still recognise that 'shit happens', but they know that the one thing we can influence is our *response* to adversity. A key lesson we learned from our *High Performance* interviews is that the best performers quickly separate the things that happen to them – many of which fall beyond their control – from their responsibility to react in the most effective way.

We are surrounded by things that we can't always control: our jobs, our relationships, our families; illnesses, recessions, global pandemics. But if you want to be a high performer, you must realise that how you react to setbacks is down to you alone.

WHY RESPONSIBILITY MATTERS

The distinction between 'fault' and 'responsibility' began with the legendary psychologist Albert Bandura. Born in 1925 to a large family of modest means, Bandura grew up in a tiny town in rural Canada. He quickly realised that success was only to going to come through hard work, self-reliance and perseverance.

When he finished high school, Bandura got a summer job filling in holes on the Alaskan Highway. While he was digging, he became intrigued by the outlook of his fellow labourers – especially those with drinking and gambling habits. His observations led to a lifelong fascination with the way our minds work. Bandura went on to study psychology at a number of universities, before eventually being offered a position at Stanford University. He spent over fifty years there exploring the science of success, eventually becoming chairman of the psychology department.

One simple, powerful idea intrigued Bandura. He speculated that when people don't believe they have what it takes to complete a task successfully, they would see little point in making an initial effort. When these people did attempt a task, their resolve would disappear as soon as they hit obstacles. He called this 'low self-efficacy'.

However, when people think they are made of the right stuff and start out expecting to do well, they are far more likely to make a start and to persevere when they do encounter difficulties – and along the way discover new ways of navigating the path to success. He called this 'high self-efficacy'.[2]

Neither is a strictly accurate way of looking at the world: in practice, we all have some control over some areas of our lives, but no control over others. But those who *believed* they could control their fate consistently fared better in life.

Bandura's research, since popularised by authors including Charles Duhigg, has transformed how the world thinks about success. Researchers have found that people with high self-efficacy tend to put success or failure down to their own actions – instead of suggesting it is the result of forces beyond their control. If they miss out on a job, they might think it's due to a lack of practice or attention – rather than the quality of the other candidates, or just bad luck. They may be wrong – it could well have been bad luck – but someone with high self-efficacy will emphasise their responsibility anyway.[3]

Today, there are heaps of evidence suggesting that high self-efficacy significantly increases your life chances. Having a strong sense of control over your life has 'been linked with academic success, higher self-motivation and social maturity, lower incidences of stress and depression, and longer life span,' according to a team of psychologists writing in 2012. People with high self-efficacy earn more money, have more and longer-lasting friendships, report having more fulfilled relationships, and feel happier about their lives in general.[4]

In short, people who took responsibility for their situation – and concluded they could influence it – ended up happier than those who didn't. Taking responsibility doesn't just boost self-esteem. It gives you greater control over your life.

Why does taking responsibility have such a positive impact? To understand the answer, we need to delve into the minds of those who feel that everything is out of their hands. And to do that, we need to examine a close relation of the notion of low self-efficacy: 'learned helplessness'.

In a series of experiments by the psychologist Martin Seligman, dogs were placed in a closed box and shocked at random intervals.[5] The dogs had a predictably horrible time, yelping and barking as jolts of electricity ran through the cage. At first, they did everything they could to get out – but the box was locked shut. (If you were thinking this experiment is more than a little cruel, you would be right.)

Yet the important part of the experiment came next. Afterwards, the same group of dogs were placed in a similar but unlocked box. This time they *could* escape the shocks – they just needed to jump over a small partition. But now, something strange happened. Many of the dogs did not actually try to escape; they simply lay down and waited for the shocks to stop. Seligman concluded that having had a series of bad experiences that they *couldn't* prevent, the dogs generalised from it – and started thinking they never had any control over anything.

You've probably met people who have a sense of learned helplessness: those who think that nothing they do can stop bad experiences happening to them. They hate their job, but they don't look for another one. They don't like their personality, but don't do anything to change it. Everything they say is negative.

Those who take the opposite approach are more likely to flourish – to get out of the box, and stop receiving the electric shocks. These people realise that their actions can change their situation – because each of us has agency over our own lives. And that's why taking responsibility is so important. If you believe you're in control of your life, you're more likely to actually end up in control.

It's a worldview that can be summarised in a simple dictum: the only person who can take charge of your life is you.

HIGH PERFORMANCE PIT STOP –
THE NO BLAME PRINCIPLE

Jake

I work on live TV. The pitfalls are many and varied. And also invisible. I often have no idea that some highly embarrassing and very public pitfall is right there. Until I've fallen in it, that is.

When Liverpool won the league in 2020, their first title in thirty years, the game was live on BT Sport and I was the presenter. We had an exclusive chat lined up with their head coach, Jürgen Klopp, moments after their victory. With millions watching at home, my producers gave the word that Klopp was ready to speak.

I knew what to do. This was just what I'd been practising for. Quieten the pundits, take a breath, excite the audience, turn to the huge screen over my shoulder and welcome Jürgen Klopp to the programme. It was one of the biggest moments of my career.

'I'm delighted to say, joining us from the team hotel, is the Liverpool manager Jürgen Klopp,' I said. Suddenly, I was standing before a twenty-foot image of the victorious manager – complete with his famous glasses, a Liverpool cap and a huge grin. 'Jürgen, you have finally done it. Can you describe your emotions right now?'

But something was wrong. Klopp's smile turned to confusion, and he started gesticulating and uttering something to someone behind the camera. He didn't look impressed.

The producer's voice appeared in my ear again: 'He's having trouble hearing us, let him go and we'll sort the issue and then go again.' I could already feel the embarrassment rising. I was well aware that during a pandemic, everything is different – we were dependent on a fallible video app like Zoom. Much of what was happening was out of our hands. But it was still frustrating.

Unsurprisingly, we didn't get Jürgen back. He immediately went to another broadcaster, gave a wonderful, tearful interview and then enjoyed the rest of his night.

The Jake from a few years ago would have dwelled on this mistake for hours. I'd want answers, and I'd want someone to blame. I wouldn't sleep, running through what had gone wrong in my head – not just for hours or days, but for weeks.

But this time, I remembered a lesson I'd learned on the podcast: the power of taking responsibility. As annoying as the technical problem was, it was my duty to react in the most constructive way. If I dwelt on the incident for days, behaving rudely and horribly to my colleagues and family, that was on me. The best solution was the simplest: instead of trying to allocate blame, I should focus on my own reaction.

I call this the No Blame Principle, and I use it every day of my life – from the smallest moment to the biggest. It seems odd at first, but try taking 100 per cent responsibility for everything that happens to you, good and bad.

As for the Jürgen Klopp interview? Well, as my wife often says: 'C'est la vie, it's only TV.'

FOCUS ON WHAT YOU CAN CONTROL

This all sounds useful in theory, but it raises some tricky questions: what have individuals with a high responsibility mindset done to develop it? And how can we all follow suit?

From our interviews with high performers, three key elements stand out. The first is to focus more on the things in your life that you can control – and focus less on the things that you can't.

On the podcast, this principle was best illustrated by the legendary Dutch striker Robin van Persie. He learned its power early in his career. Van Persie grew up in Rotterdam, and joined one of the city's major football teams, Feyenoord, as a teenager. Within a couple of years, it had become clear he wasn't just a good player – he was a world-class one. After making his senior debut at seventeen – and winning the UEFA Cup final at the end of that same season – van Persie was chosen as the Netherlands Talent of the Season for 2001–02. And, in spite of a mixed record at Feyenoord – many players and coaches thought he had a petulant, entitled attitude – nobody could deny his skill. After a few years at the Dutch club, he was signed by Arsenal in 2004.

From the moment he arrived at Arsenal, van Persie was a great fan of the club's legendary manager Arsène Wenger. 'A few minutes chatting with Arsène Wenger were enough,' he would say later. 'I knew I could trust this man. He is as crazy about football as I am.' Unfortunately, Wenger wasn't always so keen on van Persie. The manager was irritated by van Persie's repeated yellow and red cards, and was hard on him in public and in private. 'Robin's subsequent success in his career was not always obvious,' Wenger once said. 'I was very patient with him.' One newspaper report in the *Telegraph* captured Wenger's frustration, when he described van Persie as '21 going on nine'.[6]

These early years at Arsenal were a difficult time. Van Persie knew that he wasn't living up to his potential. He wasn't just immature: he wasn't playing as well as he could. Part of the problem, van Persie told us on the podcast, was that he kept allowing his opponents to get him down. 'My opponents would know how they could get me to react. They would say certain things to me or stand on my toes during a game,' he recalled. 'Anything to disrupt me and upset me. If I missed a chance, then I was very emotional and angry. My opponent would see that I'm disappointed and I'm not happy with myself and [he] grows in confidence.'

As a young player, this mindset would send van Persie into a spiral of negativity – causing him to lose confidence. And in turn, low confidence would lead to poor performance, which undermined his self-belief even more. This cycle of pessimism is a well-known phenomenon, particularly in sport. Dragging opponents into a cycle of pessimism was a skill the Australian cricket team perfected in the 1990s. They would force batsmen to recall all of their previous failures, weaknesses and mistakes by whispering to them at the wicket – a tactic called 'sledging'. Australian captain Steve Waugh would later reflect with pride on this tactic, which he said could bring about the 'mental disintegration of opponents' before a single ball is even bowled.

In his early career, van Persie was effectively sledging himself. 'I would come down heavy on myself,' he told us. The main problem was that he kept focusing on the things that he couldn't influence – his opponents, the fans' reactions, the media criticism. 'I was focused on uncontrollable factors, which meant I was mentally and physically drained after every match for quite a long time. I realised that I was constantly fighting myself and others,' he said. This tendency to blame external factors initially provided van Persie with a comfort blanket: 'It allowed me to explain away a defeat easily.'

Eventually, however, van Persie realised that there was only one way to get back on top: to focus on the things that he *could* control. It was an insight he gleaned straight from the manager:

> Arsène Wenger approached me one day in training. He asked me, 'Why are you not yet world class?' I asked him who was, and he initially said nothing – simply pointed across the pitch at Dennis Bergkamp, Thierry Henry, Patrick Viera. 'They,' he said, 'are the standard you should be at.' I was stunned. 'How do I get there? What do you suggest?' I asked. 'That,' he said, 'is for you to work out.'

Van Persie shook his head. 'It was great coaching,' he told us. Moments like this made van Persie realise that turning around his performance was in his hands alone: 'High performance is partly about how you respond to pressure – and it took me some time to realise that I was in control of my reactions.'

 'High performance is about how you respond to pressure. It took me some time to realise I was in control.' Robin van Persie

You might think that's easier said than done. But van Persie came up with a method:

> I wasn't satisfied, I wasn't happy. It was going OK, but not good enough. So I started to write a letter to myself about what I wanted to achieve at the end of my career, and how I was going to take responsibility to achieve it ... I realised I needed to stop reacting in

the manner I was. I should stand above it and respond differently.

The method was clever – it drew van Persie's attention away from the things he couldn't influence, and towards the things he could. Although van Persie might not have realised it, he was using a tried-and-tested approach known as the Zander Letter, which takes its name from the conductor Benjamin Zander. In his position as a professor at the New England Conservatory of Music, Zander was frustrated by a persistent problem: students would get so anxious about all the grading and examination that they would feel paralysed – and stop taking creative risks.

One night, he decided to find a solution. After much discussion with his wife, the therapist Rosamund Stone Zander, they decided to try something radical. They would give everyone an A at the beginning of the course. All the students had to do in return was write a letter. It must begin: 'Dear Mr Zander, I got my A because … '. It then had to describe, in as much detail as possible, how they came to achieve this 'extraordinary grade', as though it had already happened.

Zander later said that the letter worked because it made the students 'place themselves in the future, looking back, and report on all the insights they acquired and the milestones they attained during the year, as if those accomplishments were already in the past.'[7] Zander argued that this method helps people to remove the barriers to achievement – and to embrace the responsible outlook that would get pupils a real A, rather than one awarded automatically.

For van Persie, writing the letter was transformative. In the months after he wrote it, he realised his career was looking up, and within a few years, his performance had transformed.

'I truly became a top player in the years that followed,' he told us – an understatement from a man who won the Premier League's Golden Boot two years in a row and is one of Arsenal's all-time top scorers. After writing the letter, van Persie began to look at his own reaction to setbacks and ask: What can I control? Is complaining going to help, or should I focus on the things in my hands?

At twenty-four, van Persie was finally ready to understand the difference between fault and responsibility. 'Just in time,' he laughed.

HIGH PERFORMANCE PIT STOP – THE ZANDER LETTER

The Zander letter can help you, too. Write yourself a letter dated twelve months from now. This letter should begin with 'Dear [Your name here]', and should detail how, precisely, you achieved a goal that you currently have.

This visualisation of your success should not include any future tense. Phrases like 'I hope', 'I plan to' or 'I will' are not allowed. Instead, write the letter as if those accomplishments are all history, and that you're looking back at them from a distance. Be as detailed as possible, and identify the practical steps you took, and the decisions that you alone were responsible for.

At the end, you'll have a rough map to taking responsibility for your life over the next year. What lessons can you learn from the letter? What will it make you do differently?

RESPOND TO THE PROBLEM AT HAND
(NOT THE ONE IN YOUR HEAD)

James Timpson grew up in a family that fostered dozens of young people, many because their parents were in prison. The experience of helping people less fortunate than him would have a major impact on his outlook, even when he became CEO of the family business, the iconic British retailer Timpson.

The idea of employing ex-offenders and people on day release came to Timpson after he befriended an inmate who had shown him round a local prison. 'I really liked his personality so I offered him a job when he came out, and he was great,' Timpson recalled.[8] In the years that followed, he would visit several prisons on the lookout for potential employees.

But when he first suggested employing ex-offenders, many of his friends and colleagues were appalled: '*They'll* steal from you'; '*they'll* rip you off'; '*they'll* only use their salary for drugs.' People generalised about what ex-offenders are like, instead of engaging with them as individuals.

Timpson knew that this kind of generalisation was a dangerous game. He chose to ignore his colleagues' responses and went ahead with his plans, choosing to judge each situation on its own merits rather than applying sweeping generalisations. The result? Nearly 10 per cent of his workforce are ex-offenders.

Timpson's unusual recruitment policy works. Many of his ex-offender staffers are among his highest-performing employees. 'You can help people perform who've never had an opportunity to perform before,' he told us. 'But when you get it right they can be absolutely amazing.' At a time when many high-street retailers are closing down, Timpson's business continues to expand – with 2,000 stores and counting.

There's nothing better, Timpson told us, than meeting ex-offenders whose lives he has turned around: 'To me, that is the privilege of being a boss – seeing these people who when they joined you are reserved, can't meet you in the eye ... and you see them a year later and they're a manager, and the sales figures are good.'

 'You can help people perform who've never had an opportunity to perform before.' James Timpson

Timpson's experience leads us to the second way we can take responsibility for our lives: by responding to the situation at hand. All too often, when faced with a problem, we overgeneralise. Have you ever found yourself thinking, 'Nobody ever solves this problem' or 'People are all the same'? Not only is this usually inaccurate; it leads to a sense of impotence. If you overgeneralise about the problem you face, it makes you feel that there's little you can do to affect its outcome. It's a recipe for low self-efficacy.

To understand how this process works, we need to pay a visit to the top of your brainstem – nestled deep in the middle of the bottom portion of your brain. There's a system of neurons in our brainstems called the reticular activating system (RAS), which kicks into action when we start overgeneralising.[9] Among other things – looking after your sleep cycle, contributing to your levels of alertness – your RAS likes to take what you say and finds lots of examples to support it.

Say you buy a new car, a yellow Beetle, and then the next day, all you see on the roads are yellow Beetles. That is your RAS in action. In many cases, that's no problem. The RAS serves a clear function: it's what allows us to sift out what's relevant in the unmanageable amounts of information we all take in every day. Your RAS knows you're interested in yellow Beetles, and shows you where they are.

The trouble is, the RAS also applies this approach to the obstacles you face in life. For example, if you say, 'My team never has any good ideas,' your RAS will find lots of examples to support this fact. It makes us catastrophise.

In his research on learned helplessness, Martin Seligman came up with three 'Ps' that indicate you're overgeneralising. People who view their problems as pervasive, permanent and personal tend to end up with worse life outcomes than those who view them as specific, temporary and external.[10]

Let's take each of those Ps in turn. Pervasiveness is when vague, unclear and general terms like 'they', 'everybody', 'no one', 'totally', 'completely' and 'everything' sneak into our vocabulary. This was the problem that James Timpson's friends and colleagues had when they talked about ex-offenders. These can be dangerous terms because they do not require a particularly deep understanding of an issue – instead they allow us to make lazy and broad generalisations. But this problem is something we can tackle. When you find yourself thinking, 'Everything about this project is going wrong,' try to think of what elements of it (however small) have gone right. And when you spot a friend saying, 'They always do X,' try to offer up an example of when they've done Y.

Assuming that a situation is the second P – permanent – is similarly toxic. How often, when faced with a problem, do you find yourself using words like 'always', 'all the time' or 'never' ('I never get it right,' 'This always happens to me,' 'Every time I try … ')? This is dangerous. What you are doing is telling others – and, most crucially, yourself – that the problem you have is inescapable rather than short-term. Language is crucial here. Using words like 'occasionally', 'recently', 'lately' and 'some of the time' are far more empowering. They are also more accurate. Too many of us tend to take on the characteristics of tabloid journalists when relaying negativity to others – the more sensational and inescapable the better. As a result, we imagine our short-term problems to be long-term, even permanent.

Finally, we can learn to stop viewing problems as the third P: personal. When we view the issues we encounter as resulting from deep-rooted personal flaws rather than the world around us, we end up feeling helpless. If you immediately start to turn the focus inwards and blame yourself for the problem ('How could I be so stupid?'), you are making it personal – and it is rarely helpful. This isn't the same as passing the buck, or failing to take responsibility. Think back to Billy Monger: you can take control of a bad situation without thinking it's your fault. High performance is about taking responsibility for what you do; it isn't about constantly blaming yourself.

Perhaps the most inspiring example of these methods came from Evelyn Glennie. A prodigious musician from an early age, today Glennie is recognised as the greatest solo percussionist of her generation. Her performances are dizzying to watch – her hands dart across the instruments so quickly that they become a blur. All you can take in is the beauty of the music.

But Glennie has an unusual story for a musician. She is deaf, and has been since she was twelve. For some of us, losing our hearing might spell the end of any musical ambitions. Not so Glennie. She told us about a childhood music lesson in which she realised that deafness need not stop her becoming a percussionist. Her teacher struck a timpani, then let the sound hang in the air. 'He didn't say anything: he just let the journey of sound happen. And then he said, "Evelyn, do you feel that sound?" ... I listened again and I said, "Yes, I think I do."'

From there, Evelyn came to realise that she could listen to sound – even feel it – without necessarily hearing it. 'Having a hearing impairment is a medical thing. But to listen? Well, you can have a flat graph when it comes to hearing – and still be a profound listener,' she said. The vibrations travelling through the room were enough. 'It was as if my body became a huge ear.' Deafness, she suddenly realised, needn't stop her becoming a musician.

 'You can have a flat graph when it comes to hearing, and still be a profound listener.' Evelyn Glennie

We were intrigued by how Glennie came to view her disability in these terms. On one level, it was down to her upbringing: she grew up in a Scottish farming community where they 'don't make mountains out of molehills,' she said. But it was also about taking responsibility. Her deafness was out of her hands; but her response was not. 'For me it was not focusing on deafness,' Glennie said. 'I know I'm different, but nevertheless that's my responsibility – I'm not going to work with a conductor or fellow musician making excuses like, *You need to do this, you need to do that because I can't hear you.*'

In practice, that meant focusing on the immediate, practical issues she encountered – and not catastrophising. As Martin Seligman might put it, she viewed deafness as a specific problem, not a pervasive one. 'You have to be very clear what the situation is ... This is the scenario, that's what needs to happen, and it makes absolutely no difference to the quality of the end product.' That meant tweaking her behaviour – facing the orchestra at ninety degrees to better feel the vibrations, for example – but not overgeneralising about the scale of the problem.

Glennie's story reveals the power of dealing with an issue on its own terms. Deafness wasn't the end of her musical career. It was just an invitation to reappraise how she thought about music. She couldn't hear, but she was one of the most talented listeners in the world.

OWN YOUR MISTAKES

One final method helps high performers take responsibility for themselves. We all make mistakes, but it's sometimes hard to own up to them. Not so for our podcast guests: they invariably own up to their errors – even when doing so has life-altering consequences. This ability to own your cock-ups is the third way we can take responsibility for our lives.

To understand the power of this approach, it's worth examining the life of Ant Middleton. Today, many regard Middleton as an adventure hero. A former member of the elite Royal Marines, he's climbed Everest and sailed a replica of the eighteenth-century ship HMS *Bounty* across the South Pacific. He's authored a number of bestselling books and starred in several popular television series detailing the challenges of becoming an elite soldier.

To get there, Middleton had to go through a gruelling process. The first step was his Marine training. At their training camp in Lympstone, Devon, the Marines recruit members by putting them through a daunting selection ordeal, with a failure rate of up to 80 per cent. Only the best will pass. The eight-month assessment involves placing people in a pressurised environment where their reactions to instructions, understanding of briefs, leadership and team-working skills are tested to their limits.

A central part of the assessment is observing people's reaction when things go wrong. The recruiters call this 'dislocation of expectation'. The goal is to take someone and throw them headlong out of their comfort zone, then see how they respond. The Marines believe that, under stress, a person's natural state comes to the surface. In these moments, you get a sense of what someone is *really* like. Do they put themselves or their team first? Do they react to the issue at hand, or seek to apportion blame? It's all about trying to answer one simple question: would you go into battle with this person?

By the end of the process, Marines should be taking complete responsibility for their decisions – and, just as importantly, for their mistakes. That is what the course taught Middleton. He believes that his Marine training gave him a complete sense of ownership over what he did – not just on the battlefield, but in his day-to-day life. On the podcast, he explained to us how his approach to responsibility runs deep. 'When it does go wrong ... I've only got one person to look at, and that's myself,' he said. 'No excuses.'

'When it does go wrong, I've only got one person to look at, and that's myself. No excuses.' Ant Middleton

This is not just a theoretical position. For Middleton, things have been known to go very wrong indeed. In 2013, he was convicted of grievous bodily harm (GBH) after attacking a policeman on a night out in Essex. Two of his friends had got into a fight; when the police arrived, one officer allegedly started poking Middleton in the chest. 'Long story short, he knocked the policeman out, stood over him with the cosh he'd disarmed, and then went on the run, special forces-style,' the *Times* reported in an interview with Middleton. 'He was eventually found hiding moustache-deep in the River Can.'[11]

The incident still makes Middleton feel angry. 'I genuinely believed that he [the police officer] was abusing his authority,' he said in the same interview. But Middleton also realised the importance of taking responsibility for what was, let's be honest, a pretty huge error of judgement. On the *High Performance* podcast, he recounted how, before the trial, his lawyer had asked him how many tours of Afghanistan he had completed. '"Three," I told him,' said Middleton. '"The last one wasn't long ago."'

According to Middleton, his lawyer advised him that this meant he could secure a lenient sentence. If he emphasised his experiences in Afghanistan – and perhaps even said he had post-traumatic stress disorder (PTSD) – he would get off lightly. But Middleton was unequivocal. '"I can't do that," I said. "I haven't got PTSD."' Instead, he was going to own up. '"I got drunk. I had a fucking fight, and I ended up hurting someone. I deserve to be in prison. Let me do my time." And that's exactly what I did. I went to prison.'

For Middleton, this was one of the key lessons of his Marines training: you need to take responsibility for your mistakes, just as much as your successes. 'You have to hold yourself accountable,' he says. 'I made a bad life decision. I was at fault and I'm account-able for that.' He paused before adding the most important truth he had learned in Lympstone: 'You have to take responsibility.'

In the end, the incident was an unexpected blessing. Middleton describes the fight and the ensuing sentence in HM Prison

Chelmsford as 'probably one of the best things that ever happened'. It was a wake-up call, making him realise he had to straighten himself out for his wife and children. Within six years of his release, he had channelled his energies into becoming a success in the worlds of television, publishing and live theatre. Along the way, he had given up fighting altogether.

THE RESPONSIBILITY EQUATION

By now, you should be able to make out the features of a high performance worldview. High performers take absolute responsibility for their actions. They focus on the elements of their life they can control, they avoid overgeneralising in tough situations, they own up when they screw up.

We can summarise this worldview in a simple equation.

$$L + R = O$$
(Life + Response = Outcome)

Whatever happens to us – whether we're trying to become a world-beating Arsenal player or trying to complete a difficult task at work – this is what's going on. Life throws things at us and we respond; the outcome is a combination of the two.

The difference between high performers and the rest of us relates to which part of this equation they focus on. If you don't like the outcomes you're getting, it's all too easy to focus on the 'Life' component of the equation. You can blame the economy, the weather, the political climate, the 'system', and in many cases you'd be right: they all affect our lives. But where does that leave you? As you can't control any of them, isn't this just a recipe for feeling helpless?

On the other hand, high performers focus on the 'Response' part of the equation. Think about what you can change: your mindset, your language, your behaviour. In the end, this is all any of us can influence. Focusing on these factors make us feel empowered.

It took Robin van Persie a few years to work this out, but now he's anxious to pass the lesson on to his children. On the *High Performance* podcast, he shared with us a recent discussion he had with his son, Shaqueel:

> My son plays for Feyenoord under-14s and they were in a final, a big game against Ajax. He was on the bench, and he didn't play at all. In the car on the way back, he was really disappointed, complaining about others, about the coach. I pulled the car into the side and had a discussion. I said, 'Shaqueel, you sound like a loser. When you talk like this, in a way, it means you have already lost. You are blaming him, you are blaming her, you're blaming this, you're blaming everything. I don't hear one single thing about yourself.'

Van Persie's lesson was laced with love. But it had a clear – even harsh – moral. 'I'm your dad and the only job your mum and I have, is that we raise you to be a good boy, ready for life,' van Persie told his son as they drove home. 'You can make mistakes, you can do what you want – I will love you for the same amount. It doesn't matter for me if you make it as a football player or not.'

Yet Shaqueel wasn't living up to the ambitions he said he held. 'You say that this is your passion,' van Persie said to Shaqueel. 'Winners take control. They blame themselves, and they look where they can improve. This is what you should be thinking about.'

'Winners take control. They blame themselves, and they look where they can improve.' Robin van Persie

'I simply said, "Ask yourself the question: are you a loser or are you a winner?"' He concluded with a tough message: 'If you want to be a winner, take control of your life and stop complaining about others.'

The next time his son attended training, van Persie decided to go and watch. 'I saw this young tiger training, running, working hard. I was pleased. He realised he has to take control of his life.'

We can all apply this lesson in our own situations. Imagine waking up on Monday morning to the pouring rain. If you look out the window and let out a moan, that is simply a negative response to a fact. But while you can't control the weather, you can control your reaction. If, later that morning, you get stuck in a traffic jam or another driver is rude to you, that is out of your hands – but if you get irritated, or retaliate needlessly, that's on you. If you get to work to find out a colleague has been promoted (and you haven't), all you can do is be gracious in response, instead of sulking and feeling jealous.

Imagine if you chose to appreciate the wonder of the natural world when it rains, felt empathy for the other poor driver who's probably had a bad morning or decided to raise your game at work so that you'll be the next person to get promoted.

To put it bluntly: imagine taking responsibility. The 'L' has remained exactly the same. All that has changed is the 'R'.

LESSON SUMMARY

- Taking complete responsibility for yourself is the first step to high performance. No one can control what happens to them, but everyone can control their response.
- There are three steps to taking responsibility for your life. First, isolate the elements of your situation that you can control – and spend your time and attention on them.
- Second, focus on the issue at hand, and don't over-generalise. Try to think about what you can do about the problem that is in front of you.
- Third, accept responsibility when you *do* screw up – as all of us do, all the time.
- Remember what Robin van Persie told his son: 'Losers look for blame, winners look to themselves.' We can only move towards high performance by focusing on our own actions.

Building your motivation is like training for a marathon. Work at it and you'll go further than you'd ever imagined.

GET MOTIVATED

'**D**oes Steven like money?'

It was the summer of 2004, and Julie Ann Gerrard had just boarded a flight to Lisbon. She was flying to Portugal to support her son, who was playing for England at the European Championships. She found herself on the same flight as Rafael Benítez, the new manager of Steven's club. Benítez's predecessor at Liverpool, Gérard Houllier, introduced the pair to one another.

'Rafa shook her hand, said hello, and then immediately asked her a very blunt question: "Does Steven like money?"' recalled Gerrard in his autobiography, *My Story*. 'Apart from a standard "Hello, good to meet you" introduction, those were the first words Rafa said to my mum.'[1] Unluckily for Benítez, Gerrard and his mum were so close that word got back to the midfielder the moment she stepped off the plane.

Whether Benítez was joking, or genuinely trying to get into the head of his new midfielder, it marked the beginning of a chequered relationship with Gerrard. The question he asked Gerrard's mum was indicative that Benítez never quite got what was driving one of his star players.

You see, Benítez was not alone in thinking that motivation

is down to external factors only: money, fame, success. His question, however, misunderstood the true nature of high performance. If Gerrard's motivation had simply been to amass the most money in the quickest time possible, he likely wouldn't have stayed at Liverpool.

Gerrard was driven by something more essential. His link with the club ran deep. He had first represented Liverpool on its junior teams at the age of nine. When he was made captain in 2003, he became a rare thing in modern football: a local boy leading the team he had always supported.

And that meant his motivation was down to so much more than salary. 'Sometimes I would stop on the drive home from Melwood and just sit in the car and tell myself, "I'm captain of Liverpool football club,"' Gerrard later wrote in his autobiography.[2]

This deep-rooted commitment to the club paid off. At the 2005 Champions League final in Istanbul, Gerrard turned the game around with a stunning second-half header – which started the team's comeback from 3–0 down to beat AC Milan and win the trophy on penalties. At half-time he had given his team the kind of rousing speech that only someone truly committed could: 'Make every challenge count, every run count, every shot count. Otherwise you will fucking regret it for the rest of your lives.'[3]

Over the course of his seventeen-year career, the level of Gerrard's commitment to Liverpool would be tested to its limits. Just six weeks after lifting the European Cup in Istanbul, Gerrard found himself handing in a formal transfer request from his boyhood club. José Mourinho, the charismatic head coach at Chelsea, had been casting admiring glances in Gerrard's direction, and made him a generous offer – an offer that Gerrard almost accepted.[4]

But Gerrard wasn't primarily being lured by the money. The 25-year-old had found himself increasingly unhappy with his club, thanks to a disconcerting silence from Benítez in the negotiations over a new long-term contract.

It wasn't about his pay cheque – it was about respect.

As a result, Gerrard found himself on the verge of leaving the club he loved more than anything. The decision was a fraught one, and Gerrard talked it over with his family. 'I told Dad and Paul [Steven's brother] that I didn't think the club had shown me the love I needed,' Gerrard later wrote.[5]

In the end, Gerrard rejected the Chelsea offer – and the rest is history. In an interview a decade and a half later, he remained convinced he'd made the right decision – ultimately rejecting Mourinho's offer: 'I don't have any regrets about not going to Chelsea. None.'[6]

By the time Gerrard came on the *High Performance* podcast, his career had taken another turn. He was by then the manager of Rangers – a role he took on after a successful stretch coaching Liverpool's youth team, following his retirement from professional football. But the lessons he learned about motivation during his time at Anfield had stayed with him.

Gerrard's relationship with his boyhood club offers an intriguing insight into motivation. You've probably noticed that high performers seem to have an extraordinary internal drive: they seem unrelentingly committed to being their best. But we often get the source of this motivation wrong. It's easy to think that motivation is all about getting the rewards right – and with the right salary or enough prestige, we'll feel driven. This was, perhaps, Benitez's mistake when he met Gerrard's mum: he viewed motivation as the outcome of a mental calculation in which Gerrard was balancing efforts against rewards.

In fact, motivation is much more complicated. Recent research has revealed a wholly new way of thinking about motivation. It shows that true motivation is rarely about external trinkets. True motivation comes from within.

YOU'RE GETTING MOTIVATION WRONG

If you want to understand the real, hidden drivers of motivation, a good place to start is the life of Zack George.

Throughout his childhood, George was hugely overweight – eating McDonalds and family packs of sweets on an almost daily basis. 'I was probably the complete opposite to what I am now. I ate junk food multiple times a week, I hated exercise,' he told us on the *High Performance* podcast.

His parents were worried. And so they offered him an incentive to lose some weight. That incentive would be the new PlayStation. 'I really wanted the PS2,' George told us. His dad spotted an opportunity. 'My dad was like, "I'll make you a deal – I'll buy you a PlayStation 2 if you lose some weight,"' George said. 'And I was like "Oh my God, I'm gonna get a chance to get this."'

To start with, George cut out the junk food. 'Instead of having five McDonald's a week, I'd probably have three. And instead of having Haribo every day after school, I'd have fruit instead,' he said. It worked. 'After about a month, we did some measurements, and I had lost some weight. Dad was ecstatic, mum was happy, and I was really happy because I felt great about myself.'

But there was a problem. Once he'd lost the weight – and won his PS2 – George suddenly had no real incentive to keep getting fit. He had been given the treat he was looking for, and it became harder to motivate himself.

His mindset only changed when he went to a course by life coach Tony Robbins. 'It was a fantastic seminar,' George said. And it fundamentally altered his motivation:

> It was the first time where I wanted to get in shape and get healthier for *myself*. And I didn't need any external reward. I didn't need someone to say, 'Oh, I'll give you this if you do this' ... I just wanted to be happier, be healthier, and tap into my full potential.

This shift in mindset was a turning point in George's life. He soon began playing sports like rugby and squash – and rapidly came to excel at them. 'I played rugby at a high standard and realised that looking after myself actually helped with my performance,' he said in one interview. Fitness soon became his main passion. 'It was just quite a big shift mentally – to do it for myself rather than just so I could get something from it.'[7]

'I didn't need any external reward. I just wanted to be happier, be healthier, and tap into my full potential.' Zack George

After leaving school, George studied for a personal trainer qualification from Loughborough University. But his true athletic calling came when he discovered CrossFit, after his dad sent him a clip of the 2013 CrossFit Games. He immediately loved the idea of a sport that included swimming, lifting, handstand walks – everything. 'As soon as I saw it, I thought, "That's what I want to do. I want to get to the Games,"' he would say.[8] After a few years working hard at the sport, George had established a formidable reputation. At the 2018 CrossFit Open he came in at sixth place, earning the nickname 'Silverback' in the process. Two years later, George took the top spot in the UK's CrossFit Open.

You might notice that George's story has much in common with Steven Gerrard's. In both cases, our high performers were presented with an external reward – a PS2, a multimillion-pound Chelsea contract. In both cases, this was at first highly motivating. And in both cases, they eventually realised what was truly driving them to greatness came from within.

Psychologists call this the distinction between internal and external motivation. Essentially, external motivation is driven by external rewards – such as money, fame or praise – whereas internal motivation comes from the inherent satisfaction of an activity, with no rewards necessary. This distinction might sound small. But it's one of the dividing lines between high performers and the rest of us.

The discovery of internal and external motivation began with a 1971 experiment undertaken by Edward Deci, a young academic at the University of Rochester in upstate New York.[9] Deci gave two groups of psychology students a task designed to test their problem-solving skills. The students were asked to solve three Soma cube puzzles (a little like a 3D Tetris game or Rubik's Cube). After the groups had completed the second puzzle, Deci and Ryan explained that they had to leave the room to get some paperwork.

That was a lie. Instead of going to get any papers, he spent the next eight minutes watching the group through a two-way mirror. Each group spent about three and a half minutes working on the Soma pieces, he observed.

On the second day, Deci mixed it up. Group 1 were informed they would be rewarded with a dollar for each puzzle they got right. Group 2, however, were again asked to complete the puzzles with no mention of a reward. After they completed the second puzzle, Deci left the room.

This time, the group who had been offered a cash reward spent more time working on them. They seemed more motivated. On the other hand, the group who hadn't been given a reward behaved in about the same way as they had the day before. No surprises there: when you offer people money, they work harder.

More surprising was what happened on the third day. This time, Deci did something radical. Group 1 were given some sad news – from now on, there would be no financial reward for solving the puzzles. Meanwhile, Group 2 carried on as before – blissfully ignorant of the possibility of a cash prize.

Group 1 started the task as usual. But soon it became clear that something had changed. In their eight minutes of free time, they lost much of their motivation – getting distracted by the magazines littered around the room rather than working on the puzzles before them. Group 2 used the downtime to spend as long as ever working on the puzzle.

What was going on? For the group offered a cash reward, the motivation hadn't lasted. It appeared that external rewards gave a temporary boost to their motivation but the effects quickly wore off. Those who'd been offered money seemed to lose the intrinsic drive to keep working. The group who had never been offered any money at all, however, kept their motivation up across the three days.

This study, which is today one of the most-cited studies in the history of psychology, demolished the belief that the best way to get human beings to perform tasks is to give them rewards. It showed that external rewards can only get you so far. Think of these goodies like a strong coffee on a sleepy morning: it's a great buzz while it lasts, but its effects inevitably wear off.

From here, Deci – along with a graduate student he met in 1977, Richard Ryan – began to develop a new model of human motivation: one they called 'self-determination theory'.[10] Their theory states that when motivation is driven by internal, 'self-determined' forces – like personal growth and self-development – it is associated with higher levels of self-esteem and lower levels of depression and anxiety. On the other hand, when it is driven by external goodies – wealth and fame, for example – it is associated with lower self-esteem, and higher levels of depression and anxiety. Across the board, internally motivated individuals have more focus and confidence, which in turn leads to greater motivation.

An interesting insight. But only so useful. It's inevitable that many elements of our lives won't be internally motivating. Not everything you do is all that interesting. Life is defined by many dull tasks – filling in spreadsheets, attending life-sapping meetings – that are hard to get excited about. In practice, all of our behaviour is driven by a combination of internal and external drivers. Consider a moment when you have tried to get someone to alter their behaviour – encouraged a child to work harder at school, for example. You might focus on a combination of internal factors ('You might even enjoy it') and external ones ('I'll give you a piece of cake').

For that reason, it's best to think of internal and external motivation not as an either–or, but as a spectrum. Deci and Ryan encourage us to envisage a line, which ranges from 'complete non-self-determined behaviour' at one end of the scale to 'complete self-determined behaviour' at the other.[11] The extremes represent pure external motivation and pure internal motivation. All of us will fall somewhere in the middle – in fact, in the course of an average day we will move back and forth across the spectrum.

In their book *Developing Mental Toughness*, the sports psychologists Graham Jones and Adrian Moorhouse identify a variety of categories of motivation, ranging from fully internal to fully external.[12] Read through the following descriptions and reflect on where your own motivation generally lies – when you're at work, when you're at home, when you're practising a hobby.

– **Complete non-self-determined behaviour**
You work hard because you need external rewards in order to feel OK about yourself. Others' recognition is the only way to make you feel like you're doing well, and you equate your self-worth with material symbols of success. Without these rewards you are nothing.

– **Low self-determined behaviour**
You work hard because you being rewarded for your success. The rewards you get for doing something are integrated into your sense of who you are – 'I am a person who is good at X.' This gives you a strong sense of motivation.

– **High self-determined behaviour**
You work hard because you enjoy the act itself. Success gives you a sense of satisfaction, and in turn allows you to do more of the things you enjoy. There are external factors for sure – who wouldn't like a pay rise? – but, luckily enough, they are in line with what you enjoy doing anyway.

– **Complete self-determined behaviour**
You work hard purely because you love it. The joy of taking part is all that matters to you – external rewards don't feature at all. Often, when immersed in tasks like this, you forget that external rewards even exist.

Do any of those ring true? All of them? For most high performers, their motivation in their chosen field will sit in those last two descriptions. Many of their characteristics – mental toughness, the ability to bounce back from defeats and setbacks, the passion to master a craft – are based on 'self-determined' internal motivation.

But that doesn't mean there's no hope for those of us who relate more strongly to the earlier descriptions. We all experience all of these emotions at one time or another because motivation is flexible – and that's a good thing. It means that, with the right tools, we can all build ours.

HIGH PERFORMANCE PIT STOP –
MOTIVATION MATRIX

Write down a few different tasks that you encounter in your day-to-day life. Include things you do both for money and for fun, ranging from the most dull admin tasks at work to your most beloved hobbies.

Next, draw two intersecting axes. One axis spans from tasks you hate to tasks you enjoy. The other axis ranges from things you're bad at through to things you're good at. Like this:

Now plot the tasks you identified above on this graph. If you are bad at something and dislike it (our example: long, corporate meetings), place it in the bottom left quadrant. If you are good at something and like it (our example: interviewing high performers), place it on the top right.

Can you see a pattern emerging? For many people, this is the quickest way to prove the power of internal motivation. The things you enjoy – that is, tasks you find internally motivating – tend to be the ones you excel at. But just as fascinating are the exceptions. Many of us have a few skills that we hate but begrudgingly accept we're quite good at. What does the pattern look like to you? What does it tell you about your motivation?

BE TRUE TO YOU

Fortunately enough, self-determination theory doesn't just tell us that internal motivation is important. It explains where internal motivation comes from – and what we can do to build it.

After decades of study, Deci and Ryan managed to pin down the three forces that build your internal motivation: autonomy, competence and relatedness. 'When these needs are satisfied, we're motivated, productive and happy. When they're thwarted, our motivation, happiness and productivity plummet', writes Daniel Pink, whose book *Drive* offers an intriguing insight into the science of motivation.[13]

But what do these three terms actually mean? Let's take them one by one, starting with autonomy. A good example of what a lack of autonomy feels like came in our *High Performance* interview with Reece Wabara, the former Manchester City and England under 20s player, who surprised everyone when he quit football to focus on his fashion label: Manière De Voir (which means 'way of seeing').

From the outside, Wabara's football career looked like it was on the up. A graduate of Manchester City's academy, in 2011, aged just twenty, he signed a three-year deal with the club. His professional career seemed to have huge momentum.

But there was a problem. Wabara didn't enjoy the narrow strictures of professional football, either on or off the pitch. 'I was deeply unhappy towards the end of my playing career,' he told us. 'I needed to establish control of my own life.'

The problem, he said, was operating within a world in which people aren't allowed to be themselves. Wabara always had an interest in fashion and the more glamorous side of the beautiful game, but that was frowned upon. 'I was regarded as being flamboyant. People would judge me by the clothes I wore, the cars I drove,' he told us. It was draining. 'I was told that numbers don't lie, but it didn't matter how well I played or did my job, coaches would say I wasn't focused.'

After a few frustrating years, Wabara decided to do something radical: 'I grew increasingly frustrated by this lack of control, of being judged and having my career determined by those who weren't prepared to look beyond their own perceptions. Starting my business was my way of putting my destiny back in my own hands.'

Wabara started Manière De Voir in 2013, looking to build a brand that specialised in elegant high-end clothes. Eight years later, the company is an extraordinary success, turning over £1 million a week. Wabara thinks its success is down to the fact that it was his calling. 'What I've done is open to everybody ... It's just a case of being disciplined, consistent, having a path,' he told us. What made him successful, though, was that it was true to him:

> If it's not your natural calling, don't force it. I feel like a lot of people my age and younger will see that someone

is an entrepreneur, and think he seems to be making money and looks cool. They kind of force themselves down that avenue, which isn't meant for them.

Many people will be familiar with this sensation. Wabara's story reveals the first step to true motivation: autonomy. Psychologists define autonomy as acting in harmony with your sense of self – and, as Wabara's experience shows, it is an integral part of internal motivation. To be motivated, your work should reflect your core values. To be motivated, you need to be true to you.

'What I've done is open to everybody. But if it's not your natural calling, don't force it.' Reece Wabara

Why does this matter? 'The great benefit of being able to convincingly rationalise one's work as a manifestation of the true self is that it gives the individual direction and purpose,' writes Dr Sara James, whose work is explored in Brad Stulberg and Steve Magness's book *The Passion Paradox*. 'Work then provides answers to [an individual's] fundamental questions: "Who am I?" and "What should I do with my life?"'[14] If our work chimes with our sense of self, we will be motivated; if it conflicts with our sense of self, we will be demotivated.

What can we actually do to find this sense of purpose, though? On one level, this is an abstract question. Most of us have a sense that some tasks are more meaningful than others, but can't explain why. To find the solution, it's worth taking a look at the work of the psychiatrist and Holocaust survivor Viktor Frankl. He began to think about the power of meaning in horrific circumstances. In 1942, at the age of thirty-seven, Frankl had been taken to a Nazi concentration camp. The experience convinced him that even in a situation where some of the most fundamental human needs –security, shelter, food – are denied, creating a sense of purpose would help people survive. Frankl wrote that people's search for meaning – rather than pleasure, power, status or wealth – is what defines them.

By 'meaning' he meant something simple. In Frankl's view, we all want to find the answers to the question: 'What for?' We seek out a sense of purpose that transcends our particular circumstances – and contributes to something greater than ourselves. This search was about thinking 'less about what to expect from life but rather [asking] yourself what life expects of you'.[15]

We need not experience anything as awful as Frankl to heed his message. When we find a sense of purpose that is bigger than ourselves it drives our sense of motivation. Try to identify the values that you hold dearest: a commitment to your family, a desire to make the world fairer or the importance of being in a team. If we want to feel motivated, we need to focus on the activities that resonate with our sense of what really matters – and of who we are.

TAKE CONTROL

People love to be in control. From infancy onwards, much of our behaviour is simply an expression of a penchant for influencing the world around us. Toddlers squeal with delight when they knock over a stack of building blocks, push a ball or squash a cake on their head. Why? Because they did it themselves, that's why. When we can't control the world around us, it can cause us to feel stressed, unhappy, hopeless and depressed – just as Wabara's experience showed.

This is the flipside of one of the insights of Lesson 1 – focusing on what we can control. Not only does this method help us build responsibility, it also boosts our internal motivation.

Taking control of your situation – or, as Deci and Ryan would put it, exercising your competence – is the second crucial way to build motivation. According to self-determination theory, competence is about our sense of mastery of an area: we believe we are in charge, and that feels good. We can bolster our sense of competence through the very act of making decisions. 'Each choice – no matter how small – reinforces the perception of control and self-efficacy,' a group of psychologists from Columbia and Rutgers wrote in 2010.[16]

When people believe they have control over their situation, they work harder and prove more resilient to setbacks. Our desire for control is so powerful – and the feeling of being in control so rewarding – that we often try to take control of the uncontrollable. People feel they are more likely to win the lottery if they can choose their own numbers for the tickets, and feel more confident they will win a toss if they can throw the dice themselves.

Professor Mauricio Delgado of Rutgers University in New Jersey uses the example of being in a traffic jam. 'You know when you're stuck in traffic on the freeway and see an exit approaching, and you want to take it even though you know it'll probably take longer to get home?' he told Charles Duhigg. 'That's our brains getting excited by the possibility of taking control. You won't get home any faster but it feels better because you feel like you're in charge.'[17]

To understand the power of taking control of your situation, it's worth examining the career of Olympic medal-winning diver

Tom Daley. He first got interested in diving at the age of seven – after seeing older boys jumping off the high board at his local swimming pool in Plymouth. Soon, he learned he had a knack for it. Within a couple of years, he was one of the country's most promising divers; and by 2008, at the age of fourteen, he was competing for Team GB at the Beijing Olympics – the youngest member of the team.

But Daley's career hasn't always been easy. Three years after his success at Beijing, his father died of a brain tumour. A year later, he became the face of the London Olympic Games. And another year after that he came out, rapidly becoming a vocal advocate for LGBT+ rights. Soon he and his partner, Lance, became parents to a baby boy. Despite facing grief, pressure and prejudice as well as success, acclaim and love, Daley has performed with astonishing consistency, winning gold at three World Championships, as well as becoming the first British diver to win four Olympic medals, including gold at Tokyo.

How does he do it? The answer, perhaps, lies in the way he exercises control. He told us that, from a young age, he has always liked to control his surroundings. In the early years of his career, he had a cuddly toy monkey that had to travel with him to every competition. 'I know it didn't make sense,' he laughed, 'but his presence gave me a sense of comfort and helped me believe I was in control of things.' He recounted the blind panic he felt when discovering he had lost the toy. (His mother, Debbie, was sent on a frantic hunt for a replacement.)

Today, the toy monkey has been confined to history. But Daley continues to emphasise the importance of control when it comes to motivation. 'Over the last few years, I have been in the habit of starting every day by writing down three things which I aim to achieve that day,' he told us. 'It doesn't matter how big or small the tasks are. It is about following the process – controlling the things I can.'

 'It doesn't matter how big or small the tasks are. It is about following the process – controlling the things I can.' Tom Daley

At heart, it is this sense of control that keeps Daley motivated to perform at his best. 'I strive every time for performance goals – a complete set of 10s – which will help me achieve the outcome: of winning a gold medal and the personal pride and achievement that comes from that as well as the legacy which I can make,' he told us. 'To do this, however, it has to be all about the controllable elements – the process.'

Why does this method drive motivation? Because when we feel in control of our surroundings, we feel like we are competent – that we are the masters of our own fate. Take control of your situation, and you'll take control of your motivation too.

HIGH PERFORMANCE PIT STOP – HOW TO TAKE CONTROL

Damian

I have seen a few demoralised sportspeople over the years, but I can't recall a bleaker atmosphere than the away team dressing room at Twickenham at half-time on the evening of 16 March 2019.

I had worked with the Scottish national rugby team for

four years, and this match was one of the worst I'd seen. The team traipsed off the field in the midst of a hiding by an energetic England team in front of their home crowd. The score, best looked at through your fingers, was England's biggest ever half-time lead in a Scotland–England match: 31–7.

Scotland's players looked like they were in shock. As the medics and physios patched up their cuts and bruises, I was more worried about the long-term mental wounds such a defeat could bring. Over the previous forty minutes, the team seemed like their confidence had completely disintegrated.

The head coach, Gregor Townsend, was furious. His detailed instructions, thoughtfully explained over the previous week, seemed to have been discarded. He took himself and his assistants into a small room, where he could process the damage. Yet when he emerged, he delivered a mesmerising speech. Now, he appeared calm, composed and clear-headed. 'We need to forget the performance,' he explained. 'Forget the scoreboard. The game has gone.'

Instead, he shifted the players' focus from the outcome – potentially being humiliated – to the process: the behaviours they *could* control. He asked them to focus on three behaviours: being brave, taking risks and sticking together. 'Do that,' he declared, 'and we can leave this stadium with our heads held high.'

Following Townsend's speech, I watched the team focus entirely on the controllable behaviours – and, almost unbelievably, turn the game around. Scotland delivered one of the most exhilarating second halves in rugby history, scoring five tries to tie the game 38–38 – in the process retaining the Calcutta Cup.

It taught me a valuable lesson about motivation – or, more importantly, about demotivation. When you're feeling demotivated, it can help to just focus on the things that *are* in your hands. There's a story, perhaps apocryphal, about Winston Churchill in which he advocates making two lists: a list of all the things you can do something about, and a list of the things you can't do anything about. 'Do something about the things you can do something about – and then go to sleep,' he says.

This is what Tom Daley did when he was training for the Olympics. And it was what Scotland learned to do in that fateful second half at Twickenham, too. If you're ever feeling demotivated, write down all of the things that are in your hands – and cut out everything else.

FIND WHERE YOU BELONG

Before we sat down to chat with the legendary Chelsea and England footballer Frank Lampard, we found ourselves repeatedly watching a video of a West Ham United fans' forum from 1997.

In early 1996, at the age of just seventeen, Lampard had made his debut for West Ham. He seemed like the perfect player – not just a talented young midfielder, but also a local boy who had spent a few years in the youth team before stepping up to join the main club. It was surprising, then, that his arrival at the club was met with intense suspicion.

Because Lampard wasn't just any local kid. In those days, he was known as Frank Lampard Junior. Until a decade earlier, his father, Frank Lampard Senior, had been one of the club's star left-backs; and his uncle, Harry Redknapp, was the club's manager. Many fans thought that Lampard's presence in the club was down to one thing only: nepotism.

These tensions came to a head at the fans' forum, in which West Ham supporters were given the chance to ask questions of Redknapp and a panel of players – including Lampard. West Ham were underperforming, and there was a tense atmosphere in the room at Upton Park in East London with Redknapp coming under fire from the fans. Until the attention turned to Frank Lampard.

One fan takes the mic and asks a cutting question: 'I want to ask Harry if he thinks the publicity he's given young Frank here is warranted – because personally I don't think he's quite good enough yet.'[18]

The players sitting on either side of the manager make a face, and try to laugh it off. Not so Redknapp himself. 'He is good enough and he definitely will be good enough,' he says. As the fan starts protesting, Redknapp ups the ante: 'That's your opinion, and I've got the right to my opinion ... I'm telling you now – and I didn't want to say this in front of him – but he will go right to the very top. *Right to the very top.*'

We were intrigued by how Lampard had felt about the hostility of the West Ham fans – and about the support of his uncle. 'I was brought up in an area which was full of West Ham fans, where the motto in life was: always look after your family,' Lampard once wrote. And so the criticism hurt. 'I felt it in the harshest way possible. I was part of the West Ham family, literally: my nan, my Dad and Mum, my uncle and sisters. But I didn't get looked after. I didn't receive any backing ... Where was their loyalty to me?'[19]

But, thanks in part to the support of his uncle, Lampard would soon prove the fans wrong. First, he became a key player in the West Ham starting eleven. By the end of his playing career, he had been a driving force in another London team – Chelsea – that had won three Premier League titles, a UEFA Champions League title, four FA Cups, a UEFA Europa League title and two Football League Cups. Along the way, Lampard established himself as one of the greatest midfielders of the twenty-first century.

The role of his family at West Ham – and his subsequent acceptance from Chelsea – made Lampard even more mindful of the power of belonging. On the podcast, he emphasised the need to feel at home in a group that will encourage and nurture you. 'I still carry some of that East End family ethos,' he told us. 'It's even stronger now I'm a coach.'

Lampard's worldview is a neat introduction to the third way we can build motivation: relatedness. According to self-determination theory, our motivation increases when we have a sense of connection with the people around us. Humans are social animals. We know how to cooperate. This cooperation – whether taking care of the vulnerable, protecting territory or gathering food for the group – allowed for a higher rate of survival. The need to feel connected to others is programmed into our DNA.

How can we build up this sense of relatedness? One way is to try to seek out nurturing, encouraging groups of people to offer us support. Such support networks can come from the most unlikely of places – as we discovered when we met the former captain of England's rugby team, Dylan Hartley.

The interview got off to an interesting start. 'I've done plenty of these kind of interviews,' Dylan Hartley told us as he walked into the London hotel where we were recording this particular podcast episode. 'And I've eaten the interviewers up and spat them out.' It didn't take a great leap of imagination to understand how Hartley had racked up almost two years' worth of bans for foul play, missing out on the 2013 British & Irish Lions tour of Australia. 'This will be interesting,' we whispered to each other.

But once we sat down and started talking, our first impressions were confounded. Hartley was thoughtful and pensive, and shared many well-considered insights into a career that had seen him leave his home in New Zealand at fifteen, travel more than 10,000 miles across the world, and eventually captain England to two Six Nations titles and a first away series win in Australia. He was nothing at all like the aggressive player depicted in the media, who seemed interested only in fighting.

In fact, he was motivated by something greater: the sense of belonging he got from playing for a team that he loved. 'Northampton Saints has been more than just a club to me,' he said when he retired from professional rugby. 'It has been a place that has provided me with direction, purpose, a sense of family, home and belonging; and ultimately a community that I was so proud to represent every time I got a chance to play.'[20]

England's head coach Eddie Jones would come to admire Hartley's community mindedness. Jones took over the England team in 2015, when they were at a low ebb. England had just become the first ever host nation to be knocked out of the World Cup at the first group stage. One of his first tasks was to determine who should captain the team. Jones had declared that he wanted his team to become 'hard-nosed' and play a physically tough, uncompromising brand of rugby. His impression of Hartley was that he fitted this mould – 'he was a nasty bastard.'[21]

But when he actually met Hartley, Jones realised that there was much more to the man than he had expected. He had invited Hartley to meet him in a Surrey hotel. 'A chubby little bloke walked in,' Jones later wrote. 'He was bookish and wore glasses. He looked more like a fourth-year philosophy student than a rugby player.' Jones was surprised. 'Hartley offered me his hand ... He looked nothing like the ogre depicted by the media.'

Just as we did in our interview, Jones came to realise that Hartley was motivated, at heart, by a desire to build the team's sense of belonging – or 'relatedness', as a psychologist would put it. 'Beyond the fact that he was obviously a decent human being,' Jones recalled, 'I was interested in his ability to engage positively with different people. It was clear he could bring the players together.' Jones soon came to understand Hartley's ability to remind players of what really mattered. 'He was our main "glue guy" who held the team together,' Jones would write.[22]

Hartley agreed. Jones 'saw the group was fractured,' Hartley said. 'He saw me as a people person. I had a connection with everyone in the room. I worked really hard at knowing my players, having a little in-joke with everyone. He saw me as that kind of foundation captain, something to hold a team and a culture together.' Hartley soon realised had a unique knack for building the team's sense of belonging.

'I had a connection with everyone in the room. I worked really hard at knowing my players.' Dylan Hartley

And it worked. In 2019, England came as close to winning the World Cup as they had in over a decade, falling just short in the final. It was an unrecognisable performance from the team of just five years previously, and much of the transformation was down to the power of relatedness.

MOTIVATED MEANS HAPPY

At the end of our *High Performance* interview, we asked Zack George about what he had gained by making the leap from external motivation to internal motivation.

His answer was immediate. 'The main thing that springs to mind is confidence. Because I wasn't a confident kid at all, and I wasn't happy in the way I looked,' he told us. 'There's that self-confidence and self-happiness that no external award can give you.'

 'Internal motivation brings a self-confidence and self-happiness that no external award can give you.' Zack George

George's answer was the most succinct answer we had heard on *why* driving your motivation is so important. On one level, motivation is useful for practical reasons. If you want to succeed in life, you need to have a sense of drive – it's the only way to properly commit to our actions. But on another, it's about joy – and that matters even more. As George put it, 'A message I like to get across to people is that being healthy and being happy in yourself is one of the most important things in life.' This lesson doesn't just apply to physical fitness, either. If you take control of your motivation, you won't just be more successful. You'll feel better too.

As we've seen in this chapter, the secrets to internal motivation lie in a shift in mindset. The first step is to realise that long-term motivation – 'high-quality motivation', as Richard Ryan and Edward Deci put it – isn't about extrinsic goodies, like a pay rise or gaining followers on Instagram. It's about your own inner drive: the ability to enjoy something on its own terms and feel good about the rewards inherent in doing it.

Where does this internal motivation actually come from? As our high performers found, there are three ways to build this internal drive. There's Reece Wabara's discovery when he left professional football to grow his business that the most motivating things are those that give us a sense of purpose. There's Tom Daley's lesson, gleaned at the top of a ten-metre diving board, that we feel motivated when we have taken control of our situation. And there's Frank Lampard's insight from his earliest days at West Ham: when you feel like you belong, you are prepared to work harder.

What's striking about all these factors, however, is that all of them are in our hands. All too often, we think of motivation as something that's static: you're either driven or you aren't, and that means there's not much you can do to change it. The trouble is, it's a myth. None of our high performers always had these characteristics. Many learned them the hard way – think of Lampard's unpleasant experience with the fans at West Ham United. Think of increasing your drive like training for a marathon. Motivation isn't something you're naturally born with; it's something that you have to work for. But work at it and you'll go further than you'd ever imagined.

That's why building your motivation is such a crucial step on the road to high performance. There are so many elements of our life that fall out of our control. Getting motivated isn't one of them.

LESSON SUMMARY

- While material rewards and social status can drive motivation in the short term, they're rarely enough in the long run. True motivation comes from within.
- Internal motivation comes from three sources. First, 'autonomy'. When your behaviour aligns with your values, it's easier to get excited about it.
- Second, 'competence'. We are most motivated when we have control over what we're doing.
- Third, 'belonging'. When we feel part of something bigger than ourselves – like a team – we can sustain our motivation for longer.
- The value of internal drive goes far beyond motivation, however. It's good for your whole world-view – like Zack George, motivated people are happy people, too.

Eighty per cent of victory is in the mind.

MANAGE YOUR EMOTIONS

L et's start this chapter with a quiz.

You're going to read three accounts of high performers working under pressure. In each case try to guess: what happened next?

1. **Chris Hoy**
    Date: 1 August 2003
    Location: Hanns-Martin-Schleyer-Halle Arena, Stuttgart
    Event: World Cycling Championships

The 1 kilometre might just be the hardest event in cycling. It requires acceleration and speed, but, like the 400 metres in running, there is also an endurance element. Chris Hoy, probably Britain's greatest ever cyclist, once described the event as 'gladiatorial'. 'You have one chance,' he said. 'Your body is on the line and it's cruel because everyone cracks. The trick is to crack later than everyone else.'[1] The words of the American cyclist Sky Christopherson are even starker: 'My blood was turned into battery acid.'[2]

Hoy had won the event in 2002's World Championship in Copenhagen. The following year, he travelled to Stuttgart to defend the title, his confidence bolstered by the thoroughness and rigour of his preparations at the team's Manchester base.

The set-up of the kilo seems almost designed to ratchet up the pressure. Each competitor waits patiently for their turn, watching while each of their rivals makes their attempt – and their own start draws ever nearer. As defending champion, Hoy was scheduled to race last.

In the race that immediately preceded his, Hoy watched his German rival, Stefan Nimke, break the 1 kilometre time trial world record. The crowd's response was ecstatic.

What happened next?
A. *Hoy blasted out of the blocks to shatter the fresh world record and retain his world crown.*
B. *Hoy tied with Nimke, and the two men shared the title.*
C. *Hoy choked, couldn't get his speed up properly and came a disappointing fourth.*

2. **Kelly Holmes**
   Date: 8 August 1995
   Location: Ullevi Stadium, Gothenburg
   Event: World Athletics Championships

Kelly Holmes is one of the greatest British Olympians of all time. Her performance at the 2004 games in Athens marked one of the most dramatic comebacks in modern Olympic history – when Holmes confounded all expectations to win gold in the 800 metres, despite being thirty-four years old and approaching the end of her career. The image of Holmes' stunned face upon realising she had won the 800 metres is famous, often described as one of the most iconic images of the modern games.[3]

But by the time of her victory in 2004, Holmes had long been one of Britain's greatest runners. A seminal early moment in her career came in 1995, when she entered the World Athletics Championships in Gothenburg. Then still a serving member of the British Army, Holmes was on top form. She had won every race she had entered that year. 'I approached the championships with confidence, determined to go for gold,' she would later write. 'I knew I had a good chance of winning.'[4]

The only runner she had not faced was Hassiba Boulmerka, the women's 1,500 metre world champion in 1991, and Algeria's first ever Olympic champion in 1992. Boulmerka had been injured, and the World Championship was her first competition of the season.

'We were drawn in the same heat and we ran quite different races,' Holmes recalled. 'Boulmerka ran close to the front from the start, whilst I stayed at the back waiting for my moment. I came in a comfortable second behind her. When the draw for the semi-finals were made, it was announced that we were racing each other again.'[5]

Holmes' long-time coach, Dave Arnold, publicly complained that the two rivals had been drawn together twice before the final. In this second race, both athletes battled down the finishing straight, shoulder to shoulder. Boulmerka eventually inched ahead to beat Holmes by 0.02 seconds.

The next day, they would meet again in the 1,500 metre final.

What happened next?
A. *Holmes stormed down the final straight to win her first gold medal of the World Championships.*
B. *A photo finish was required to work out who had won, Holmes or Boulmerka.*

C.   *Holmes lacked energy and trailed home a disappointing second.*

3.   **Ant Middleton**
     Date: 2007
     Location: Helmand Province, Afghanistan
     Event: Undercover Royal Marines mission

The first time Ant Middleton was involved in a proper firefight was during a tour of duty with the Royal Marines in Helmand Province. He had been in the Marines for just two years, and was only twenty-seven years old. With eight years of service in the Royal Engineers under his belt, he was already on track for leadership.

But it wasn't easy. On one occasion, he was leading a group of men on a mission to track down a Taliban commander. 'I ran up to the door and got into position, with my teammates lined up behind me. Bullets from an AK47 – maybe more than one – started flying out of the door.[6] Milldeton's job was to run through the door the moment the bullets stopped.

What happened next?
A.   *Middleton was the first man in, dispatching enemies quickly and efficiently – just as his training had taught him.*
B.   *He stormed through the doorway, but the mission wasn't as successful as he had hoped because the enemy combatants had made a quick escape.*
C.   *Middleton froze, and found himself unable to move through the door; he had to be supported by a colleague.*

What do you think? The answers might surprise you.

1.   **Chris Hoy**

Correct answer: C

Hoy underperformed and finished a disappointing fourth, well behind the medal winners. 'I felt like a kitten, but was trying to pretend to be a lion,' Hoy explained. 'Instead of thinking logically about how Nimke had gone so fast, I panicked and abandoned my strategy, and my form quickly followed. I changed my plans and set off way too fast, which caused me to mess up towards the end.'

Hoy described the experience as a 'huge psychological blow.' On the *High Performance* podcast, he told us that all manner of doubts began to set in: 'I wondered if I had peaked. I wondered if I had already been the best I would ever be.'

2.   **Kelly Holmes**

Correct answer: C

Holmes came an underwhelming second in a slow race.

'On the day of the final, a weird thing happened to me,' she later recalled. 'From the moment I woke up, all I could think about was the race. I couldn't get it out of my mind.' Normally, she explained, she had a knack for putting a race out of mind – deeming it needlessly anxiety-inducing. But this time, something was different. 'When I woke at 7am, I found myself thinking, "only 10 and half hours to go and it'll be over,"' she recalled. 'I couldn't stop the thoughts of the race going around and around my head, using up so much nervous energy.'

Boulmerka was in second place until the final bend, when she made a break for pole position. 'I left my response a fraction too late and couldn't quite catch her,' recounted Holmes. 'In the last few seconds of the race, my legs had gone and she proved herself the stronger of the two of us as she stormed home to win.'[7]

3. **Ant Middleton**

Correct answer: C

Middleton froze and was unable to execute his team's plan. 'What was happening to me? My legs were like concrete,' he later wrote. 'I was literally paralysed with fear.'

It was only the intervention of a comrade that convinced Middleton to move. As he stood there in terror, Middleton recalled, 'My pal behind me reached around, squeezed my shoulder as if to say, "Don't worry, Ant. When you go through that door, I'm right with you."'[8] Only after his friend's intervention did Middleton find himself able to act.

Three elite performers, three testing situations, three struggles. It is a reminder that even the great success stories of our generation can lose their cool just as we do.

What distinguishes our high performers is how they reacted to that moment of struggle. As we saw in Lesson 1, it's not our fault what happens to us, but it is our responsibility to respond effectively. All three of our high performers came back from their failures, and worked hard not to repeat them.

In each case, that response involved trying to take control of their emotions. We all want our days to be filled with thoughts and feelings that are helpful and productive, and fewer moments that make us want to run away, cry or question ourselves. In practice, though, everyone's life is filled with hundreds of ups and downs – and if we can't respond to this turmoil effectively, we will come unstuck.

And so, in this chapter we'll learn about how our emotions can trip us up – and how high performers learn to control them. This isn't about ignoring your feelings, or covering them up. It's about developing a constructive response to the harmful emotions – fear, anxiety, anger – that we are all familiar with.

On the *High Performance* podcast, we asked Holmes how much her physical skills mattered compared to her mental skills. Her answer was immediate: twenty–eighty. 'In the 2004 Olympic 800 metres final, there was 0.2 seconds which divided the top four finishers,' she said. 'Our talent was roughly equal. We could all run fast, we were all as strong and as tough as each other.' And so 80 per cent of victory is in the mind. The difference lay in how some responded to the anxiety and pressure: 'I had been taught some big lessons about adrenaline and controlling my nerves.

'You need adrenaline, but too much and you are lost.' Kelly Holmes

'You need adrenaline to gear up for a race, but too much and you are lost. In 1995, I hadn't learned to control my nerves at that stage. When I won gold in 2004, I had.'

YOUR ANIMAL BRAIN

What is going on in our heads when we freeze under pressure, or feel so anxious we underperform? To understand it, you need to get to know your brain.[9]

The most basic facts about your brain can make the thing hurt. It consists of 100 billion cells, each of which connects with up to 10,000 others. That adds up to 1 quadrillion connections – that's 1,000,000,000,000,000 – underpinning everything that we do.[10] The Nobel Prize-winning biologist James Watson once described the human brain as 'the most complex thing we have yet discovered in our universe.'[11]

Over the last few million years, this lump of tissue has evolved to protect you from trouble. It makes an almighty fuss to warn you when shit is about to hit the fan – or when it thinks it is, anyway. The trouble is, much of that fear is unnecessary – in fact, provided you live in a relatively safe environment, it can be outright unhelpful.

To understand why, we need to go on a whistle-stop tour of your brain. If you can remember your school biology, you might recall that the brain was initially explained via the 'triune model'. Like many neurological models, it works better as a metaphor than as an accurate description of how the brain works, but it's good enough. The theory, devised by Paul MacLean in the 1960s, divides the brain into three core parts – three brains in one, if you like – that mirror our evolution.[12]

According to the brain surgeon Andrew Curran, the best way to get to grips with the triune model is by using your hands.[13] Wrap one hand round the clenched fist of your other hand, and hold both in front of you. Roughly – very roughly – this arrangement of your hands represents your brain.

First, let's focus on the brainstem – represented by the wrist on the lower hand. It is at the top of your spinal column (your lower arm). The earliest part of our brains to have evolved, the brainstem is responsible for involuntary functions like your heart rate and breathing. Here, we're more concerned with the other function of the brain stem: the five 'Fs' – fight, flight, flock, freeze and, er, sex. Each is bound up with our survival. When we feel threatened, our brain provides us with three options: hide, confront the danger or run. The examples of panic shared by Chris Hoy, Kelly Holmes and Ant Middleton reveal moments when their brainstems were in control.

The second part of the brain to evolve was the clenched fist – or, to give it its real title, the cerebellum, commonly known as the 'little brain'. You can think of this as the next level up from the brainstem: it deals with deep-rooted emotional reactions, though not quite as unconscious as those of the stem. It reacts only to drives and instincts, which you experience as your most base emotions. If this system ran the show, you'd impulsively react to whatever you faced without thinking of the long-term consequences of your actions. You'd probably steal a lot of the things you liked, and murder the people you didn't.

And finally, there's the hand on top – the cerebrum. It is disproportionately huge in humans compared to other animals. It evolved last. If you picture a brain, all gooey and crinkly, the cerebrum makes up all those squiggly lines. These are folds: as our neocortex grew in size, evolution squashed a large surface area into a small space. Those grey waves were the result.

Your neocortex is responsible for all voluntary movements and your interpretations of the information coming into your brain, plus all the 'higher' functions – speech, reasoning, learning and abstract thought. The neocortex drives the more human elements of our behaviour. It gives us a social conscience, and makes us want to work with and help others. It also looks to apply logic. The neocortex enables you to think about thinking – metacognition – like you are as you're reading this.

If we want to understand how we respond in moments of high pressure, we need to get to grips with the way these three parts of our brain interact. Your unconscious, primal brain and your conscious, rational brain argue with each other. A lot. Humankind has always been aware of the tension that exists between these functions. The ancient Greek philosopher Plato said that in our heads we have a rational charioteer who has to rein in an unruly horse that, 'barely yields to horsewhip and goad combined'.[14] For our purposes, all that matters is that they pull us in different directions: the brainstem telling us to freeze or flee, our cerebellum driving our intuitive, emotional responses and our neocortex desperately pleading for us to keep calm and think rationally.

The psychiatrist Steve Peters, whose psychological advice helped turned British Cycling into a medal factory without parallel, has a useful TEDx talk that explains how this pans out in practice. Peters worked with Chris Hoy on keeping calm under pressure. In his lecture he explained what goes on in inside our brains, especially in stressful situations. Speaking to a group of schoolchildren, he used an example they might find relatable – a schoolgirl overhearing her classmate talking about her behind her back. How would the different bits of the child's brain react?

Amygdala: KILL HER!

Orbitofrontal cortext: Hang on, don't kill her yet – we have to be socially aware. So let's do it deviously, all right? ...

Dorsolateral prefrontal cortex: I'm not interested in emotion – just give me the facts and the evidence ...

Ventromedial prefrontal cortex: I don't know why we're all 'Me, me, me'. How about the other person? Let's think with empathy and compassion.[15]

As Peters puts it, 'These brains are fighting each other – and one of them has got to get control.'[16]

Overall, your brain is like a busy office: including the show-offs and bombastic bullies (amygdala), the quiet, head-down workers (ventromedial prefrontal cortex), the office geeks (dorsolateral prefrontal cortex) and the people who stick up for and protect the office geeks (orbitofrontal cortex). It's like a huge, persistent game of tug of war. Millions of years of evolution mean that different parts of your mind are continually vying for attention – and, sometimes, throwing you off course.

RED BRAIN, BLUE BRAIN

Fortunately enough, it is possible to get our noisy brains under control. None of our high performers – Chris Hoy in Stuttgart, Kelly Holmes in Gothenburg, Ant Middleton in Helmand – were undermined by their emotions for long. In fact, they all went on to achieve greatness.

The first step in this process is to develop a simple model to make sense of what's going on in our heads. In moments of high pressure, it's not very useful to think about your brain's inner workings in too much detail. None of the high performers we interviewed solved their emotional problems by saying to themselves, 'There goes my uncinate fasciculus again.'

Instead, most of the high performers we have met developed a neat shorthand to make sense of their minds. Former England rugby coach Clive Woodward referred to the T-CUP model (thinking correctly under pressure).[17] Steven Bartlett, the award-winning social media entrepreneur, employed the framing of the Nobel Prize-winning economist Daniel Kahneman: fast, emotional 'system 1' thinking and slow, rational 'system 2' thinking.[18] Some, like Chris Hoy, used the distinction adopted by Steve Peters, between the impulsive 'chimp brain' and the rational 'human brain'.[19]

But our favourite is the distinction adopted by the New Zealand rugby team following their work with world-renowned psychiatrist Ceri Evans. He talks about the emotional, impulsive part of our minds as the 'red brain', and the conscious, rational part of our minds as the 'blue brain'.[20]

Our emotional red brain holds the greater influence. 'It is neither good nor bad. It fulfils essential functions, but it is also powerful – and prone to panic,' as Chris Hoy put it. In fact, Hoy says, it is five times stronger than our rational minds. 'I learned to treat it with respect,' concluded Hoy. 'We are not responsible for the nature of it but we are responsible for managing it. As I discovered in Stuttgart, when it is left to dominate, it can result in bad decision-making.'

 'Your emotional brain is neither good nor bad. It fulfils essential functions, but it is also powerful – and prone to panic.' Chris Hoy

Your blue brain, on the other hand, is the part of you that can actually think. It's driven by facts and logic, and is motivated by compassion, honesty and self-control. It acts with a conscience, searches for a purpose in life and works for a sense of achievement.

Many of our high performers came to conclude that the only way to perform under pressure is to get your red brain under the control of your blue brain. It's not easy. In the past twenty years, studies in neuroscience and cognitive psychology have shown that your red brain is bestowed with the power to fiddle with our biochemical processes, via neurotransmitters such as dopamine, serotonin, oxytocin, acetylcholine and noradrenaline. These neurotransmitters flood your system. They bully your blue brain, getting your attention and compelling you to act.

The second step in controlling your emotions is learning to spot when your red brain has become too dominant. There's an easy method of doing this. Ask yourself, 'If I were looking at this situation from the outside, would I think that reaction is helpful?' When your red brain is filling your body with anxiety-inducing chemicals, it's difficult to see things objectively. This question allows you to get outside yourself and assess whether your response is as constructive as it could be. If the answer is 'no', your red brain probably has too much sway. But don't worry: the very act of noticing when your red brain is in charge is a useful step towards reducing its power.

That leads on to the third step in getting our brains under control. We need to remind ourselves that it's our blue brains we should be listening to. To do so, we need to develop a sense of perspective, to ensure that we're not constantly falling into an easily panicked sense of 'fight or freeze'.

Richard Lazarus, one of the most influential psychologists to study how our thoughts affect our emotions, suggests that this sense of perspective is key to feeling calm under pressure. Our red brain feels most vulnerable when we feel that we lack the resources to cope. But in many cases, we *do* have the resources to cope – we just need to remind ourselves of them.[21]

Whenever you're faced with a task, on a subconscious level you're grappling with three big factors. Say you're applying for a job and you're not sure if you've got a good shot at it, if you're ready for the step up or even if you're able to write an application. In practice, you're reflecting on the following points.

- *Demands*: What is required of me to do this job? How hard is it?
- *Ability*: Do I actually have the skills to pull the job? How does it correspond with the things I'm good (and bad) at?
- *Consequences*: What is actually at stake here? What would getting (or not getting) the job mean for the rest of my life?

We are most likely to remain calm when the demands are low, our ability is high and the consequences are not too significant. Alas, many situations don't fulfil these criteria. The results are distress, anxiety and a reluctance to take risks.

However, if we can get a sense of perspective in each area – and approach the demands, our ability and the consequences more rationally – then we can get our red brain under control. Our high performers have useful tips in each area.

WHAT IS DEMANDED OF YOU?

When we feel trapped and under pressure, developing a clearer sense of what is actually needed from us can prevent us from feeling overwhelmed.

The critical thing is to take a step back and think about what a task *really* involves. We can learn to think rationally, not emotionally, about what we're facing. Rather than the situation controlling us, we can put ourselves in control.

But how? One useful suggestion comes from Chris Hoy. Three weeks before he won his first gold medal at the Athens Olympics in 2004 – and a year after his disappointing performance in Stuttgart – Hoy was summoned for a talk with Steve Peters. Hoy told us about it on the *High Performance* podcast: 'Steve started gently, asking me how things were. "Oh, it's going really well," I said. "I'm injury free, my form's good. I regained my world title and will be starting as the number one seed at the Olympics in three weeks' time." I really was dead happy.'

Peters responded with a question. '"I want to pose one scenario: what's going to happen if someone breaks the world record just before you get to the track?"'. Hoy was surprised. 'I told Steve I hadn't thought about that. He said, "You should envisage that so it doesn't overwhelm you." At first, I replied, "Well, I just won't think about it." "Don't think about a pink elephant," he instructed. What was the first thing that pops into my head? A pink elephant! I thought, *right, well he's got my attention already.*'

'What should I do then?', Hoy recalled asking. 'Well, you can't not think about something,' Peters replied. 'But you only want to think about one thing at any one time. And if you say, "Don't think about something," you get drawn towards it. So, you have to actively choose what you want to think about. And that will displace any other thoughts.'

This insight details the most effective way to deal with overwhelming tasks. Think about what is required of you, and run through how you will respond in your head. In the process, you'll get a clear sense of what the task before you actually entails. 'You can control the momentum cycle rather than let the momentum overwhelm you,' as Hoy explained.

 'You can control the momentum cycle, rather than let the momentum overwhelm you.' Chris Hoy

Hoy described to us how, during the next three weeks, he consciously began envisaging what would be asked of him at the Olympics:

Whenever I was anxious or stressed about anything – not just cycling – I visualised the perfect performance from my perspective. It took about a minute. The first time I tried this was back in my room. I logged on to the internet and saw that one of my rivals had posted some great time in training. 'Oh God, he's going really well,' I thought. 'He'll be flying in three weeks' time.' Then I remembered, 'Don't engage with this negative thought. Shut my eyes, visualise my own race.' After a minute, I felt better and moved on.

As the race became increasingly imminent, this trick became even more helpful: 'As I got closer to the games and the pressure began to increase, I was doing this more and more. On the night itself, there was so much stress, I was in an almost constant loop of visualising my race.'[22]

The final moments of build-up are described with nail-biting intensity in Richard Moore's excellent book *Villains, Heroes and Velodromes*.[23] He captures the febrile atmosphere in the 6,000-strong velodrome as five riders vied for gold in the Olympic final. Hoy was up last, and watched the other riders nervously from the sidelines.

First up, the Australian Kelly. He stormed around the track and burst through the finish line in a new Olympic record. The old Hoy might have panicked; but the new Hoy didn't. Instead, he visualised what was imminently required of him: *I'm in the saddle, breathing deeply, leaning forward, gripping the bars, pulling back, lunging forward.*

Nimke went next. This time it was personal: Nimke had bruised Hoy's confidence at the World Cycling Championships just a year previously. This time, Hoy wouldn't let him. Nimke speeded around the track, smashing the record that Kelly had set just moments previously; but Hoy was in his own world. *I'm in the saddle, breathing deeply, leaning forward, gripping the bars, pulling back, lunging forward.*

The Dutchman Bos started badly and didn't recover any momentum. His time wouldn't alter the final placings for medals. For Hoy, though, that was irrelevant. *I'm in the saddle, breathing deeply, leaning forward, gripping the bars, pulling back, lunging forward*

Arnaud Tournant, possibly the best kilo rider the world has ever seen, came next. He started with pure, unbridled aggression, storming up the track, his enormous legs jabbing the pedals in a dizzying blur. When he crossed the line, the reaction in the velodrome was one of stunned belief. He recorded the first ever sub-61-second kilo – and a new Olympic and world record.

But Hoy didn't see it. He was busy getting ready – and reminding himself of what he needed to do.

And then, suddenly, it was his turn. Hoy sat in the saddle. He breathed deeply, leaned forward, gripped the bars. He lunged forward.

1 minute 0.711 seconds later, it was over. Hoy had set a new world record. Afterwards, Hoy circled the track in a daze as the crowd cheered ecstatically. 'I couldn't absorb it,' he said afterwards. 'I had spent so many hours visualising the ride, then it went exactly like I had rehearsed it, I thought it wasn't real.'[24]

But he had learned a powerful lesson. When a task feels too demanding, just try holding what is actually required in your mind's eye. In that moment, something that once seemed impossible becomes real.

HIGH PERFORMANCE PIT STOP – PICTURE THIS

Jake

There are times in all of our lives when we just know we have to take a leap.

For me, one of those moments came in 2010, when I took one of the biggest risks of my life to found my first start-up. The idea for the company originated from an observation from my time covering Formula 1 for the BBC. During almost every race, various team sponsors would present us with content they had filmed. They all had great access to drivers, wonderful cars and stunning locations. And almost every time, the content was rubbish – badly shot, no decent narrative, poor sound. Each video represented a wasted opportunity.

So, my brilliant colleague Sunil and I took the matter into our own hands. We decided the only way to make that content better was to create it ourselves. And we created our business, Whisper, to do just that.

The whole enterprise was a huge risk. I was putting my reputation – and cash – on the line. For Sunil, the stakes were even higher: he was walking away from a steady job at the BBC to create the company. It didn't help that we had no office, no history, no infrastructure, no staff – and, from a business perspective, absolutely no idea what we were doing.

Unsurprisingly, it was a stressful time. During those early weeks at the company, every day was chaos, and every night was sleepless. Would anyone take us seriously? Would we land any deals? Would we make enough money to pay the bills, let alone Sunil's salary?

How did we get through it? Well, this was years before I interviewed Chris Hoy for *High Performance*. Yet a big part of the answer lay in a similar method to the one he described on the pod. Every day, we learned to focus on the specific things that were being demanded of us – delivering a pitch, seeking out a new partnership, producing a video. By visualising these small things, I learned to stop myself panicking about the big things.

With time, our cool heads paid off. Our first big success came when the Williams F1 team took their own leap and commissioned Whisper to produce some content. I will never forget leaving their factory, pulling up at the first lay-by and climbing out of the car to do a jig of delight by the side of the road. It was on that journey we decided we might actually need an office. We went big right away, and decided to operate from two separate HQs: Sunil's attic and my spare bedroom.

Today, Whisper is one of the fastest-growing production companies in Europe, with offices around the world, over 150 staff and turnover in the tens of millions of pounds. But whenever things get too stressful, I think back to the method I learned in those early days: visualise what is actually required of you, and cut out the rest.

WHAT ARE YOUR ABILITIES?

By the time she turned twenty, Dina Asher-Smith was already the greatest-ever British female sprinter. Her record was unprecedented: setting new British 100 and 200 metre records in 2015, at the age of nineteen, only to smash both records four years later. But it hasn't always been easy. Asher-Smith has been open about how, in her early career, she was undermined by a fear of failure.

Her internal battle had become particularly pronounced during the World Athletics Championships in 2019. She was the clear favourite to win the gold medal for the 200 metres – and the pressure was overwhelming. 'In the semi-final, my start was appalling,' she told us. 'I was like a snail.' That poor start brought on that all-too-familiar sense of panic.

Fortunately enough, Asher-Smith knew who to speak to. She turned to her coach, John Blackie, the man who has guided her through her entire career. 'He is like a second dad to me,' Asher-Smith told us. 'His intelligence and patience is what gets us through. He knows me so well and understands my moods. He has known me since I was eight and he's had such a part to play in who I am as a woman today. I needed him badly then.'

Sure enough, Blackie had a suggestion. His idea related to the second area we need to tackle if we want to take ownership of our emotions: reminding ourselves of our abilities.

Asher-Smith told us how their conversation had unfolded. 'I was seriously panicking because this was the focal point of my career and I was thinking that the way you set up your semi-final often dictates how the final goes,' she explained.

'"That start wasn't good," I said.' Blackie agreed that it wasn't her best. Asher-Smith fired out questions like machine-gun bullets: So, what are we gonna do? Are we going to practise blocks? Are we going to get ready for the next race?

Blackie remained unfazed, his voice calm and even. '"You're going to go out next time and just do your normal start," he said. "That is all you are going to do. Just go there and do the normal start you have done thousands of time before."' The effect was instant, Asher-Smith told us: 'It was a very powerful tool. He reminded me that what I already had within me was what I needed to win.'

'He reminded me that what I already had within me was what I needed to win.' Dina Asher-Smith

'What I already had within me': these simple words hint at the second powerful tool we can use to put our blue brain back in control. When we feel overwhelmed by a task, it is easy to lose track of our abilities. We think we don't have what it takes to overcome a problem. In many cases, that's because we've lost track of what our skills actually are.

'In those big moments, many people feel like they have to outperform themselves and do the best that they've ever done to win. But psychologically, that's not the best way to go into it,' Asher-Smith told us. 'You don't have any evidence to build on. John knew that I just needed to be reminded to have a bit more confidence in my own ability. His simple message – just go out there and do what you normally do and it will be fine – was perfect.'

The next evening, Asher-Smith delivered a ninety-one-step athletic masterpiece. As she sped around the final corner and powered down the home straight, the crowd roared – knowing they might just be watching sporting history. She crossed the line in 21.88 seconds: gold was hers.

We can all use Asher-Smith's technique in our own lives, even if we aren't quite gold-medal athletes. Everyone has skills, but in moments of panic it's all too easy to forget them. One way to overcome this problem is to start actively cataloguing your abilities: what are you great at? What skills do you have?

You can imagine this method as a confidence bank account.[25] Every time you achieve something, try to recall in detail how you achieved it: how you were feeling, what you were thinking, how you behaved. In particular, focus on the skills you needed to pull it off – and try to put them into words. Becoming actively aware of the qualities that have got you to where you are is like depositing money in your account. The more you do so, the healthier your balance will be.

This becomes especially useful in moments when your confidence deserts you, just as Asher-Smith found. She got through it because she reminded herself of her abilities. 'The most important thing about my relationship with John is that I know, hand on heart, that he wouldn't let me do anything or he wouldn't put me in a position that I didn't have the ability to handle,' she said. 'He always says this same thing to me: "If I say you can do it, that means I know you have the ability to do it." That is a big confidence boost for me.'

If we have built up a comprehensive database of our capabilities, our achievements and our strengths, this allows us to make quick judgements under pressure – rather than wasting our mental energy obsessing over what has gone wrong. When we lose our way, dipping into our confidence account of previous successes helps reorient us. It reminds us what to do next and reassures us that we have what it takes.

WHAT'S REALLY AT STAKE?

Jonny Wilkinson has won a Rugby World Cup, four Six Nations, and two Heineken Cups. He has scored more points in tests than any other Englishman. His name will forever be synonymous with *that* moment in 2003 – when his left foot was the difference between England winning the Rugby World Cup and returning home empty-handed.

But the journey hasn't been easy. 'I've always suffered with anxiety,' he told us when he sat down for his *High Performance* interview.

On the podcast, Wilkinson began to dictate the terms of the conversation with grace and aplomb – just as he did on the rugby pitch. But he didn't want to discuss moments on the field.

He wanted to take us on his inner journey of self-discovery, a trip which challenged us to consider the toll of chasing high performance.

Wilkinson told us that, by the time he was playing profession-ally, his relationship with rugby had become unhealthy. From a young age, he felt 'a sense of doom about being alive', he said. His solution was to become a perfectionist: 'I created this idea that by being perfect, that would be my saving grace. And, as a result, I then unfortunately had a ridiculous passion for competitive sport. So now I'm going into competitive sport with a need to be perfect.'

This desire to be perfect would take a huge mental toll. 'Before games, and after games,' he told us, 'I had a crippling fear of this idea that what I was about to go through, or what I'd already been through, would define me.' And, as his career progressed, this pressure only built: 'The crazy thing was, no matter what I'd been through, how many kicks I'd missed, the next game held the opportunity to rid myself of that ... So I just put more and more pressure on the next game.'

The result was that he could rarely enjoy the things he was experiencing – even at the height of his career. He told us about winning the World Cup in 2003:

> You think it's amazing. The immensity, the ecstasy of that moment. Incredible. But within three or four seconds it's on the decline. There's no lasting nature to it. And then two months later you're in big trouble, because now you're way down at the bottom of the hill, looking back at your glory days.

As his career went on, Wilkinson's struggles with his mental health would become more extreme. The mental and physical pressure 'built and built and eventually exploded,' he recalled.

Needless to say, the pressure had a negative effect on Wilkinson's performance. 'The first time I got a serious injury, I didn't stop and reflect on why I got it, all I could think of was, *I've got to get back to where I was*,' he recounted. 'I allowed no room for freedom, liberation or healing. So I end up with another injury. *Oh, it's even worse now.* Each game, some big comeback – I've got to get back to where I was, instead of explore what I could be.' Wilkinson suffered fourteen consecutive injuries until he 'finally started to pay attention'.

Wilkinson's story reveals some crucial insights into the risks of obsessing too much about success and failure. It's all too easy to develop an exaggerated sense of the consequences. For Wilkinson, performing at the highest level took on a world-defining significance; failing to live up to his ambitions would have been shattering.

Worse, the more you try to stop focusing on negative conse-quences, the more important they seem to become. Worry and anxiety are our brain getting fixated on trouble that might lie ahead of us. Our attention gets dragged into the future. Regret falls into the same category, except in this case our mind gets stuck on the troubles of yesterday. As our attention is pulled forward into the future, or backwards into the past, we lose track of what really matters – the present.

The crux of the problem is being unable to accept a particular outcome: losing, making a mistake or, in Jonny Wilkinson's case, failing to live up to perfection. Our red brain is simply doing its job and refusing to allow us to ignore a threat. But often, these threats aren't as great as we think. When we come under pressure, we can develop an overblown sense of how bad the worst-case scenario actually is.

However, solutions are at hand. It's possible to develop a clear sense of which consequences matter – and, more importantly, which ones don't. Towards the end of his career, this is what Wilkinson managed to achieve. 'I learned to let go,' he told us. 'I let go of old ideas about who I am and what I had to do, what I was expected to achieve.' It was about learning to rationally answer the question: how much is really at stake?

We can all learn from Wilkinson's example. Although it is useful to set optimistic targets for ourselves, our level of attachment to them is crucial. If we can't accept anything other than the ideal, we are signing ourselves up for a tsunami of worry.

One trick is to emphasise that who you are and what you achieve are not the same. The more we identify with our successes, the higher the stakes and the more our sense of self is at risk if things don't go our way. Instead of being someone who sometimes wins and sometimes loses, we become a winner or a loser. As Wilkinson put it, 'If I choose to be a World Cup winner, because I once won a World Cup, that's going to be my next limit. If I do *this*, it means I am *this*. If I do *that*, it means I am *that*.'

However, we can develop a more reasonable approach to our achievements – one that construes our life outcomes as separate from our sense of self. Wilkinson worked hard to uncouple his identity from his achievements. This allowed him to develop a more balanced idea of what was at stake, even in the most high-pressure moments.

Even now, when working as a pundit for the rugby matches he once played in, he seeks to offer a different perspective. 'Our focus needs to be on learning from our performance instead of applying a sweeping judgement of it,' he said. He told us that he's learned to stop fixating on prestigious trophies, laughing that today he takes as much joy from doing the washing-up as from winning the World Cup.

This doesn't mean that we stop being serious about winning. We can still aim to perform at a high level. But we must learn that winning isn't the be all and end all. 'This approach doesn't mean that you stop training, doing everything you can to win,' said Wilkinson. 'It means the opposite. You explore your training. You explore your rest. You explore your own body. You explore your own being. You explore everything. And if you're exploring, you're going to find something new.'

 'You explore everything. And if you're exploring, you're going to find something new.' Jonny Wilkinson

But along the way, you learn that the stakes aren't as high as you thought. Who you are and what you achieve are not the same. Much more important is the journey. As Wilkinson told us, 'If you spend this life growing and exploring, it seems like a reasonable journey. And if you're exploring what's on the inside, it's a damn good journey.'

HIGH PERFORMANCE PIT STOP – DAC ATTACK

By now, you should have a three-part framework for understanding your red brain. When you start to panic, it's down to the interaction of three forces. There are the demands – namely the sense that the task before you is impossible. There are your abilities – in particular, the sense that yours aren't enough. And there are the consequences – all too often, an overblown sense of what is at stake. Demands, abilities, consequences – or 'DAC' for short.

Fortunately we can address each of these areas of concern by thinking them through methodically. The goal is to reduce your sense of the demands, increase your belief in your abilities and balance your view of the consequences. This exercise will help you do so.

Think of a problem that's making you anxious, and then draw out the following table. On the left are the three factors sending your red brain haywire; on the right are the crucial questions you can ask yourself to get your blue brain back in control.

The Problem	The Solution
Demands	What is actually demanded of you? Can you break it down into simpler steps?
Abilities	What abilities do you have that can help? What problems have you overcome before that required similar skills?
Consequences	What is really at stake? In a year, how much will this problem matter? Am I catastrophising about how much it matters?

Fill in the boxes on the right, with one or two sentences given over to each question. The goal here isn't to underplay your problems – some of the answers may well be a little disconcerting. But it should give you a clearer sense of what is actually going on in your head. It's a quick-fire method to get your blue brain back at the wheel.

THE LONG ROAD TO INNER CALM

Chris Hoy in Stuttgart. Kelly Holmes in Gothenburg. Ant Middleton in Helmand Province. Even the world's highest-performing people have moments of panic – even moments of crisis.

Yet all of these high performers have something in common. They developed mechanisms that allowed them to get their red brain under wraps, and used them to remain in control.

If these high performers can get their red brains in check, so can you. But it won't be easy. At its heart, the process involves discipline: knowing what's going on in your red brain at moments when you feel the pressure rising – and actively practising keeping a cool head. The only way the exercises in this chapter will come in handy is through repetition.

But, as the example of our high performers show, when it comes to becoming your best you have all the time in the world. After all, nine years after that fateful day in Gothenburg Kelly Holmes won gold at the Athens Olympics. It was almost a decade after his disastrous World Cycling Championships that Chris Hoy would cement his reputation as one of Britain's greatest ever Olympians, in London in 2012. And it was eleven years after his first tour of Helmand that Ant Middleton climbed Everest.

If there's one lesson to take from this chapter it's this: the road to high performance is long. You don't need to get there right away, and even if you fail, you'll have chances in the future to succeed.

Getting your red brain in check isn't something you can do in a day. It involves rewiring how you think about success and failure, your abilities and your weaknesses. But, with time, it's something we can all learn.

LESSON SUMMARY

- Getting to grips with our emotions is a crucial ingredient of high performance. The goal isn't to supress our feelings, but to react to them with a clear head.
- The human brain is prone to panic. But it doesn't have to be. We can prevent our emotional 'red brain' overpowering our rational 'blue brain'.
- But how? When a situation feels overwhelming, first work out what is actually required of you. Take a deep breath and ask: is this really as hard as I'm making out?
- Second, remind yourself of your abilities. What skills do you have to solve this problem? How have they come in handy before?
- Third, reflect on what is at stake – the consequences. How much does this really matter? Is the worst-case scenario as bad as you think?
- These methods take practice, but don't lose hope. The road to inner calm is long, but with time you'll reach its end.

High Performance Behaviour

Stop fixating on what you're bad at. All that matters is what you're great at.

PLAY TO YOUR STRENGTHS

Here's a situation that many parents will find familiar. Imagine your child has come home with a school report card. They show you the following grades:

English: A
Social Studies: A
Biology: C
Algebra: F
Maths: C
French: B

Is there a grade that immediately jumps out at you?

The polling company Gallup once investigated this very issue.[1] Researchers set out to examine how much parents focus on their children's best grades rather than their worst. The researchers were interested in whether we tend to be optimistic or pessimistic, when presented with information that was both good and bad. The results were striking. The survey, carried out across multiple countries and cultures, found that the majority of parents in every country immediately focused on the F.

Country	Focused on As	Focused on Fs
UK	22%	52%
Japan	18%	43%
China	8%	56%
France	7%	87%
USA	7%	77%
Canada	6%	83%

The moral is simple: people tend to focus on the negative. In one study, a group of psychologists reviewed people's responses to over 200 newspaper articles and concluded that one general principle holds true: bad news grabs and holds our attention more than good news.[2] This shouldn't be a huge surprise. In the media, 'good news' and 'bad news' have pretty much the opposite meanings to in the real world. For a journalist, a 'good news' day is filled with mayhem, murder and mischief; a 'bad news' day is when nothing in particular happens.

From reading the last chapter you might have guessed that these doom-and-gloom instincts are powered by our red brain – ever vigilant to possible threats, sounding the alarm even when it isn't necessary. It makes us focus on problems rather than opportunities.

But high performers know that this is a flawed approach to life. If you want to be your best, you need to start from the opposite end of the scale. Stop fixating on what you're bad at. All that matters is what you're great at. Find it, and run at it.

That's just what this chapter will teach you. We'll offer a toolkit for working out what your strengths are, and making them a central part of your life. In the process, we'll take you from the first pillar of high performance – how high performers think – to the second pillar: what high performers do.

MULTIPLE INTELLIGENCE

Howard Gardner, a pioneering developmental psychologist, spent his life obsessing over one question. He wondered what would happen if you took two people with wildly different lives – say, a Wall Street trader in New York and a nomadic shepherd in the Sahara Desert – and swapped their places. Both might be highly skilled in their own world, but would either of them thrive in their new environment? The answer, he suspected, was no.

This insight led Gardner to develop a theory about the nature of skill and intelligence. There's not just one form of intelligence, he argued, but many. In some scenarios, your particular brand of intelligence might be helpful; in others, it might be useless. Gardner rephrased the old question 'How clever are you?' and tweaked it to be, 'How are you clever?'

Gardner's research ultimately gave rise to his multiple intelligence (MI) theory, which argues there are many different ways to be smart. Some people have interpersonal intelligence – they have a unique knack for working out others' feelings. Others have spatial intelligence – a nous for visualising the world in three dimensions. Yet more have linguistic intelligence – they can put even the most abstract of ideas into words. These are only a few examples. In fact, Gardner identified eight different kinds of intelligence. There could be many more waiting to be discovered, he said.[3]

This insight is helpful for anyone trying to master high performance. As Gardner put it, the multiple intelligence theory can offer a 'useful inventory' – it allows us to work out what we're good at, and then pursue that above all else. In our interviews and research, we've learned how high performers disregard what they can't do, and instead structure their lives around what they can.

This was especially true among interviewees who described formal education as a process of endurance rather than enjoyment. Many didn't excel academically, and this concealed their true – perhaps hidden – forms of intelligence. Two high performers in particular demonstrate the importance of working out your strengths beyond the classroom: Jo Malone and Steven Bartlett.

Of the pair, Jo Malone's talents were perhaps the most idiosyncratic. She had a tough start in life. Growing up on a council estate in Bexleyheath, Malone told us how she spent her childhood on the edge of poverty, 'having to think about where the next meal was coming from at the age of eight'. Her father had a gambling habit; when Malone was thirteen years old, her mother suffered a stroke. Malone left school in her early teens, with no qualifications, to care for her.

But even at a young age, Malone had glimpsed what her career might be. 'I always believed that there was something else out there,' she told us. The seeds of her future success were planted early. Before her stroke, her mother had worked for a beautician called Madame Lubatti. 'I was eight or nine and I'd go to work with my mum and watch this incredible woman in the laboratory. I'd watch how face masks were made, watch Madame Lubatti grind the sandalwood,' Malone said in one interview.[4] Soon, she got involved herself, pouring the finished skincare products into pots for Lubatti's clientele.

Malone clicked with the job immediately. She proved to have an exceptional knack for creating cosmetic products. She is dyslexic, and recalls struggling to follow a formulation. However, by watching the process, she was able memorise what went into any one product.

But Malone wasn't happy working on someone else's creations – she wanted to develop her own. Eventually, in her early thirties, she launched her own range of bath oils. By 1999, when

Estée Lauder bought her company, it was a multimillion-pound business, and more than thirty years later it remains one of the world's best-known perfume brands.

Malone's story reveals that we can find our skills in unlikely places. She was always an unorthodox perfumer. Upon buying Malone's company, executives at Estée Lauder asked to see her formulations. 'I said, "I haven't got a formulation, I make it from my head,"' she told one interviewer. 'I sat in their laboratories and they'd ask me to make something, and off I'd go. They'd say, "Stop, stop! How many drops was that?", and I'd say, "I don't know! Until it feels right!", and we'd have to start all over again.'[5]

Malone's story reveals the often hidden nature of intelligence. Malone's success arose from her discovery of an unusual skill: a remarkable, intuitive grasp for making cosmetics. This isn't to say that her success was solely down to her knack with perfumes. On the *High Performance* podcast, Malone described an uncanny knack for business strategy, visualising the future steps for her company 'like a chessboard', as she put it. But the origins of Malone's empire were more unorthodox – during those early days with Madame Lubatti, and her discovery of a peculiar, and valuable, strength.

If Malone's story reveals the power of working out extremely precise 'hard' skills, then our next high performer reveals the power of finding more wide-ranging – but no less important – 'soft' skills. Whereas Jo Malone had little choice but to leave school young, Steven Bartlett just never quite gelled with formal education. His teachers described him as a 'lovely guy but a hopeless student', he told us. 'I was expelled from school when I was sixteen, when my attendance had hit 30 per cent.' The problem wasn't that he was insolent, just that he didn't enjoy studying. As he summarised it in one interview: 'Everyone thought I was going to fail in life.'[6]

However, Bartlett did have skills – just not ones that were tested in the classroom. 'There is no qualification or A-Level for managing 700 people when you're twenty-six years old,' he once said. This ability to relate to people and understand them is what would eventually make Bartlett a millionaire. 'I would be naive to say I didn't take anything from school,' he noted. 'The main thing I took was understanding people and the way they think.'[7] This, in the language of multiple intelligence, is classed as an interpersonal strength: possessing high levels of insight into how others think.

'The main thing I took from school was understanding people and the way they think.' Steven Bartlett

From an early age, Bartlett drew upon this skill for spotting what was driving people and used it to make money. 'The reason I was expelled and wasn't going to school was because I was preoccupied running various businesses,' he told us. 'One of the businesses was for the school. I was responsible for all the school trips and events for sixth form when I was sixteen.'

Eventually, even the teachers realised he had an entrepreneurial talent. He had been saving the school's finance team cash, speaking to vending machine suppliers to get them a better deal. 'It got to the point where the school had given me a whole wall in the school just to advertise events or things that I'd come up with,' he said. Later, he began setting up social nights for under-eighteens in his hometown, Plymouth: one evening 3,000 people turned up.

This knack for spotting what people around him wanted – and turning those desires into business opportunities – would eventually help the business he founded, Social Chain, take off. Today, the social media agency has a roster of clients including Apple, McDonald's and the BBC, helping each better engage with social media users. It is a $300-million social media company, with 700 staff based in six offices in Europe, Asia and the USA.

Bartlett and his team pull it off by working out which content is going to gel with people – and which isn't. It's the same intuitive grasp of what people liked (and disliked) that Bartlett had discovered at school. He had found his strength, and with it his calling.

THE GOLDEN SEED MOMENT

The trouble is, it's not always easy to work out what our strengths are. Some people go a lifetime without discovering where their true skills lie – especially when what they excel at isn't tested at school, or formally monitored in the workplace. That's why it's imperative that each of us thinks hard about what we are good at – and uses it as the basis for our high performance journey. But how?

Here, too, Kelly Holmes has some crucial insights. Sixteen years on from her famous double gold at the 2004 Olympics, Holmes sat down with us and told us her story. Her journey to sporting greatness hadn't been easy. In the course of her interview, she told us about issues at school, feeling lost as a teenager, traumatic sporting injuries and her struggles with mental health.

But through it all, she learned to thrive. And from her story we were able to glean a simple method for finding your hidden strengths. We can distil the process down to three stages:

recognition, reflection and rhythm. These principles will provide you with a framework to work out what your strengths are, too.

Let's start with recognition. The psychologist Sigmund Freud called this 'the golden seed' moment.[8] Many of us remember moments in our youth when we're told that we that we had a special talent. It might have been by a teacher, boss or family member. And gradually, over the years, we came to view this skill as a crucial element of *who we are.*

Many high performers we interviewed recognised the moment this 'golden seed' was planted. For Marcelino Sambé, principal male lead dancer of the Royal Ballet, it was the psychologist at his youth club – in one of the poorest suburbs of Lisbon – who noted the sheer pleasure on his face during dance lessons. For Eddie Hearn, the boxing promoter, it was an early fascination for marketing, combined with the encouragement of his businessman father, which fired his passion for promotion from an early age. For Shaun Wane, the head coach for England Rugby League, it was the kindness and gentle understanding of the family of his future wife, Lorraine, which stood in stark contrast to his own brutal experiences at home. These experiences made him want to create a nurturing environment wherever he ended up – ultimately for his players.

Kelly Holmes described the effect that just such a moment had on her. Her early life had been difficult. Her mother, Pam, had Kelly when she was a teenager. Her father left before she was a year old. Pam's parents encouraged her to give her daughter up for adoption, worrying that Pam was too young to raise a child alone. So Holmes spent her childhood going in and out of care homes. On the *High Performance* podcast, she recalled the moment, indelibly marked in her memory, when 'the adoption services came, literally to take me away with another family'.

Like many of our high performers, Holmes was no academic prodigy. 'I was not academic at all at school, at all,' she told us. But in her early adolescence, she realised that she had a gift. 'When I was thirteen, I took part in my first cross-country race. Despite the low expectations which surrounded me in many areas of my life, I did well.'

This led to her golden seed moment. It was all down to Holmes' PE teacher, Debbie Page. 'People often credit inspirational teachers they have had at school, those who fired them with enthusiasm for a subject in a way that influenced the rest of their life,' Holmes wrote in her autobiography. 'For me, that person was Debbie Page. She was tall, imposing, full of energy and great at her job ... Coming second in that [cross country] race was one of the turning points in my life, because it made her notice my potential and encourage me to keep running.'[9]

Having her potential noticed made Holmes try harder to be a runner. On the podcast, she explained to us the effect that identifying and labelling her abilities had on her performance. Up until that point, 'I just felt useless all the time,' she told us. 'Until athletics took its hold, and suddenly I'm winning everything.' The effects on her performance were astonishing. Suddenly, her peers and teachers were telling her she was special – saying, 'If you're going to be good, you've got to start focusing ... But you're better than everybody here.' The golden seed was planted, and soon started to grow. 'I was just like, *Oh my god, somebody's actually told me I can be good*,' Holmes laughed.

Why do these golden seed moments matter? Well, psychologists have long argued the very act of labelling a behaviour makes us inclined to commit to it. In one study by the psychologist Robert Cialdini, two groups of adults were interviewed by pollsters in the run-up to an election. The first group were told, they could be classed as 'above-average citizens likely to vote and participate in political events'. The other half were told they were about average in terms of their likelihood to vote. In reality, these two labels were assigned at random. But the effects were huge. The respondents labelled as 'above-average citizens' ultimately proved 15 per cent more likely to vote in the election.[10] They had been told they were something; and so they became it.

There's a valuable lesson here. When people tell you that you have a skill, take note. Label the skill, and seek out opportunities to use it. These golden seed moments are important; they are the first hint of what might be your calling.

HIGH PERFORMANCE PIT STOP – SPOTTING THE SEED

Jake

When I started my job at Rapture TV in the 1990s, I had no idea what I wanted to do with my life. As I mentioned in the introduction, I ended up working in TV through sheer chance, following my humiliating A-Level results. I didn't realise it would be the beginning of a career. Yet twenty years later, I believe my time at Rapture offered me my golden seed moment.

It wasn't that I had some remarkable knack for TV production. I was the lowest rung on a tiny ladder. I would spend my weekends cleaning the studio, operating the autocue, answering the phones and making tea – all for £5 cash every Sunday evening. But my time at Rapture did help realise what I *was* good at.

It all began when Rapture ran a competition for viewers to send in a home video, and win the chance to present a TV show in Paris.

The thing to know about Rapture is that we didn't actually have many viewers. And so the competition was a flop – nobody entered. And that was where me and the fellow work experience kids came in handy. To make up for the lacklustre response from our basically non-existent audience, we were asked to create some videos and to 'enter' the competition. I borrowed my friend Stephen's camcorder, and set to work.

Looking back, the video was comically amateurish. I told 'viewers' about my love of Natalie Imbruglia, filmed myself playing with my dog Dylis in the garden and showed off my rather strong Norfolk accent. But when I showed it to the producer, Roger Farrant, he was impressed. He decided to broadcast the audition, and the viewers 'voted' for me to win. I had just nailed my first audition.

A few weeks later, there I was walking down a Parisian street, talking to a TV camera. I loved it. It was the first time I had really felt in my element, nailing my links and managing to remember all my lines. The teenage me thought that I was pulling it off with tonnes of charisma. The whole set-up felt so natural.

It might sound small, but coming in the wake of my disastrous A-Level results, the praise from my producers – and that chance to prove myself in Paris – went a long way. Soon, I was trying to finesse my presenting style, and thinking hard about what our viewers (OK, our 'viewers') would like to hear about. It was a classic golden seed moment: a point when someone told me I had a skill, which led to me labelling and finessing that skill.

These days, when people tell me they're professionally stuck, I ask them to think back to their own golden seed moment. What sticks in their memory from their youth?

Was there a point when someone they respected told them they had a talent? Is that skill something they can use today?

SUCCESS LEAVES CLUES

By themselves, golden seeds are not enough. Left without water and sunlight, it's all too easy for your seed to whither. After all, many of us have talents in youth that subside with time.

So, if we're serious about working out our strengths, we need to remain vigilant – and keep checking that we're focusing on what we're great at. This leads on to the second principle of finding your strengths: reflection. High performers are constantly monitoring the areas in which they're excelling, as well as those in which they're underperforming. If you have a natural knack for something, you'll see the evidence for it all around you. Success leaves clues.

The need to think rigorously about our strengths is down to a troubling phenomenon: when it comes to assessing our own strengths, our gut instincts are often wrong. It's all too easy to think we excel at something when we really, really don't.

This is something McArthur Wheeler learned the hard way. In April 1995, Wheeler became a cause célèbre when he robbed two banks in Pittsburgh, Pennsylvania, only to be caught within a matter of hours. Why was he captured so quickly? Because the hapless Wheeler had robbed both banks in broad daylight, and hadn't bothered to wear a mask or any other form of disguise. His image was captured on the security cameras dotted around the banks, and there were plenty of eye witnesses who quickly confirmed his identity.

His problem was that he thought he was invisible. He had rubbed his face with lemon juice, having read that it was used in invisible ink. If this approach worked for ink, he thought, why wouldn't it work for skin?

This tale of comic incompetence intrigued David Dunning and Justin Kruger, professors of social psychology. It inspired them to explore the psychology of misplaced confidence. How many of us were, in our own small way, behaving like McArthur Wheeler?

Dunning and Kruger asked 194 students to undertake a series of logic and grammar tests, and then asked them to predict how they had performed compared to their peers.[11] Their findings were remarkable. Participants were poor judges of their own performance. They systematically overestimated their ability. In the grammar tests, participants tended to estimate that they were better than two-thirds of other students. Most strikingly of all, the discrepancy between estimates and reality was starkest among the weakest students. The worst quarter of students were more likely to guess that they were in the top third.

The experiment helped Dunning and Kruger develop a hypothesis. The Dunning-Kruger effect suggests that assessing how good you are at a task, and actually being good at that task, often require the same skills. So, if you have a skill, you'll probably realise you have a knack for it. But if you lack that skill, you probably won't realise you *don't* have a knack for it.

Take driving. The best drivers will know exactly why they rate themselves so highly; they can see what distinguishes them from the rest. Unfortunately, the worst drivers won't even be able to recognise the skills they lack – so may well think they're highly skilled, too. As Dunning pithily puts it, 'The first rule of the Dunning-Kruger club is you don't know you're a member of the Dunning-Kruger club.'[12]

The Dunning-Kruger effect poses a problem for anyone who wants to be a high performer. What we think we're good at and what we're actually good don't always align.

The solution is to scrutinise what you're good at – and to do so with ruthless objectivity. Kelly Holmes shared her own methods with us. She consciously revisited her successes and failures, trying to work out what she excelled at and what she didn't.

She told us about having a particularly tough patch in the late 1990s and early 2000s. By 2002, Holmes had endured a seven-year period during which she couldn't get fully fit. Ruptured calves, a torn Achilles, stress fractures, glandular fever – her ailments got worse and worse. Then, in 2003, she got injured once again, in the run-up to the World Championships. Holmes couldn't take it any more. 'I just kept thinking, everything was knocking me back,' she told us. 'I had a massive breakdown, literally to the point that I didn't want to be here anymore.' Holmes described to us the moment, in a French hotel, when she realised she couldn't carry on as she was. 'I looked in the mirror and everything inside me was just like this explosion of hatred, emotion, disappointment,' she said. 'I felt like somebody was literally wanting me to fail, like literally saying, *you're not going to do this.*'

Thankfully there were people around Holmes who could support her. Around this time, she approached Margo Kane, an American coach based in South Africa, to take over her training. 'I needed to do something different to break the cycle I had found myself in,' she wrote in her autobiography. Kane suggested a distinctive method that might help Holmes get out of her rut: 'One of the first things Margo asked me to do was write down a list of my strengths and weaknesses, my best and worst behaviours.'

'There was no doubt in my mind that my biggest weakness was my lack of confidence.' Kelly Holmes

This exercise proved illuminating for Holmes, who said she was 'in the habit of beating myself up pretty regularly'. The list of strengths ran to two pages – ranging from determination and discipline to courage and concentration. 'I could only list two weaknesses: injuries and lack of confidence,' Holmes wrote. 'There was no doubt in my mind that my biggest weakness was my lack of confidence.'[13]

This simple exercise had a profound effect. It allowed Holmes to work out what she was good at (a long list), and it helped her realise that her weaknesses – especially her responses to her injuries – were manageable.

What does Holmes' method teach the rest of us? Well, it indicates the power of explicitly identifying your strengths and weaknesses – writing them down, reflecting on them, revisiting them whenever you encounter a setback. When you're unsure of your strengths and weaknesses, take a step back and ask: what does the evidence tell me?

HIGH PERFORMANCE PIT STOP: RÉSUMÉ REVISITED

When you apply for a job, you brag about your greatest strengths: 'I am an enthusiastic team player'; 'I get on well with people'; 'I am unusually hard-working.' You usually keep these skills at the forefront of your head until the moment you leave the interview. At which point you immediately forget about them.

This is a shame. Because this method – thinking about your skills, labelling them, occasionally boasting about them – is a powerful tool for working out your strengths.

Consider writing a résumé for the rest of your life. For this exercise, we want you to write down three big achievements from the past year – and reflect on how you pulled each one off. For example, if you've written down winning a bike race, endurance might have been key. If you've wowed a big client at work, that might be down to your excellent interpersonal skills.

But, at the same time, there is often one factor that unites all of your achievements: your determination to win, or your discipline in getting the task right, for example. Is there one skill that underpins all of your accomplishments? Remember, success leaves clues – what characteristics unite your successes over the past twelve months?

FIND YOUR FLOW

So far we've focused on two ways to identify your areas of high performance: listen out for what other people say you excel at, and keep an eye on the skills that hard evidence indicates you excel at. But there's something missing: enjoyment. More often than not, the areas you excel are the same ones you find pleasurable.

To understand why, we need to delve into the research of the Hungarian-American psychologist Mihaly Csikszentmihalyi (pronounced six-cent-mihaly). As a student at the University of Chicago in the early 1960s, Csikszentmihalyi developed an obsession with the link between enjoyment and focus. When he was working on a paper he found interesting, he realised that he could become completely lost in it – and this sensation of complete immersion was uniquely exhilarating. Herein lay the origins of one of the most influential psychological discoveries of the past hundred years.[14]

In his TED Talk, Csikszentmihalyi describes how he began to properly develop his theory when he embarked on a unique study, travelling the world to find out what makes people happy. He and his team spoke to hundreds of individuals, from rock climbers to painters. The researchers developed a methodology called the experience sampling method, in which they sent a message to a group of experimental subjects eight times a day, asking them to write their answers to several short questions in a booklet. The questions touched on how they felt, what they were doing, and who they were with. It soon became an unusually comprehensive database of information on people's moods and skills.

Soon, Csikszentmihalyi noticed something peculiar: that excellence at many tasks is linked with a particular state of mind, which he christened 'flow'.

Many of us will have seen people in flow – watching an elite sportsperson at play, or observing a musician performing. When you are in this state, you are completely lost in a task. According to Csikszentmihalyi, indicators of flow include the look on your face, your breathing patterns and the amount of muscular tension in your body. Think of a pianist performing in a concert: every part of their body is given over to playing – they seem overjoyed by the complete focus that it requires.

This flow state, Csikszentmihalyi says, is when we are happiest. Just as importantly, it's when we do our best work. When we are in flow, we are completely lost in the rhythm of a task, and so we are able to produce work that is of a higher quality. The lesson is simple: if you want to play to your strengths, you need to find the tasks that bring you flow.

We've found that when you start asking high performers about their mindset in moments of complete concentration, they describe a state of flow – even if they aren't familiar with Csikszentmihalyi's research. They talk about being 'in the zone', or only being able to think about the game; they speak of the joy of complete concentration.

As ever, Kelly Holmes' example is illustrative. She recounted the experience of winning her first Olympic gold medal: 'In the 800 metres final, I started in lane three and felt completely focused, felt really good from the moment I stepped on the track. At no stage did I think about any other runner, like I had in the past.'[15] Or consider Steven Gerrard, describing getting lost in football on the *High Performance* podcast: 'I always found my best performances were when I went on to autopilot, committed everything and let it go.' Or listen to Jonny Wilkinson's definition of high performance: 'Absolute engagement ... You're either fully attentive and engaged, or you're not.'

'High performance means absolute engagement. You're either fully attentive and engaged, or you're not.' Jonny Wilkinson

The trouble is, flow isn't something you can just turn on and off. As Wilkinson acknowledged on the podcast, there are all too many moments when we start fixating on the past and the future, and struggle to truly enjoy the moment. So, what can we do to identify the tasks that make us flow?

The trick, according to Csikszentmihalyi, is to find the right balance of skill and challenge. Tasks that induce flow aren't too easy, nor are they too difficult. They stretch our abilities, but we can just about pull them off. Think of an athlete competing in a hard race, but one they know they can win, or an entrepreneur giving a high-pressure pitch, but one they're confident they can deliver. This balance of difficulty and achievability produces a degree of satisfaction that allows people to live in the moment. They feel utterly in control.

So the third principle of finding your strengths is this: try to recognise the moments you're lost in the rhythm of a task. And attempt to make the tasks that induce this sense of flow a central part of your life. The things we lose ourselves in are the things that we're good at. If we want to play to our strengths, we need to learn to spot moments of total immersion.

HIGH PERFORMANCE PIT STOP: FLOW CHART

You might be thinking: How on earth am I supposed to do that? Well, here's a simple tool to work out what gets you into flow. Sit down with a pen and paper, and draw a Venn diagram composed of three overlapping circles. Next, give them the following labels: *Tasks I find challenging; Tasks I do well; Tasks I enjoy.*

As we've seen, these are the three pillars of flow – those moments in which we are stretched but know we can pull off our goals, and in which we feel completely immersed.

Now, write down some of the tasks you undertake in your average week. Add a few more you undertake only occasionally. Place them in whichever circle – or whichever portion of the overlapping circles – makes the most sense.

Most of us find that only a few tasks fulfil all three criteria. We might find some tasks challenging, but also intensely

frustrating (for your authors: anything involving maths); we might enjoy some tasks, but we don't find they stretch our abilities (for your authors: watching Netflix).

But most of us have a few tasks that fall in the middle of the diagram – they stretch us, we can pull them off and we enjoy the process. Think about how you feel in these moments. Were you in a state of flow?

YOUR NATURAL ADVANTAGE

'I loved going into work every day at Cardiff. Good people, and I absolutely loved it. But it just wasn't me.'

We were sat beside a pitch that had hosted some of the greatest players in football history: Manchester United's training ground in Carrington, on the outskirts of Manchester. Opposite us was a man who, over the previous few years, had done more than anyone to guide these players: Ole Gunnar Solskjær, then eighteen months into one of the toughest jobs in football.

But Solskjær didn't want to talk about his triumphs as manager of Manchester United. He wanted to talk about his troubles as manager of Cardiff City. Four years before taking the top job at United, Solskjær had received a call from Cardiff, asking if he wanted to be their new manager. It was a high point in his career as a manager – his first time leading a Premier League club. But he had been unsuccessful. In the course of Solskjær's first six months, Cardiff struggled to gain momentum, eventually finishing twentieth in the league and being relegated. Solskjær didn't last a year.

Half a decade on, Solskjær was able to ruefully smile about the experience. 'That situation – it didn't suit me,' he said. 'I think maybe, as you say, you get "found out".' Solskjær had previously spent eleven years as a striker for Manchester United, serving under Alex Ferguson. He had wanted to bring the dominant, aggressive style of play that he had learned at United to Cardiff. But it didn't work: 'The style of play that we wanted to play didn't suit the players ... I couldn't go through with it.'

Solskjær's confession was the most succinct demonstration we had heard of the importance of playing to your strengths. Solskjær was undoubtedly one of the greatest football minds of his generation – not just one of Manchester United's great goal-scorers during the late 1990s and early 2000s, but also the triumphant former manager of the Norwegian team Molde, whom he had taken to their first domestic league championship. But in an environment that didn't match up to his strengths, Solskjær encountered setback after setback.

One of the most important concepts in economics is 'comparative advantage'. It means that everyone in the world gets the best results when they focus on what they're good at. In economic terms, that means if a country has extensive coal reserves, it should focus on exporting coal; if it has lush, fertile land, it should grow crops. By focusing on your strengths, the theory goes, everyone ends up richer.

We can apply this theory to our own lives. Solskjær had a comparative advantage in managing aggressive, attacking teams. Put at the head of a more conservative club, he struggled. The same was true of Kelly Holmes, who excelled at running but never at school, and Steven Bartlett, who had a great business mind but no knack for focusing in the classroom. This isn't something to be ashamed of – it just means we should play to our comparative advantage.

That's why finding your skills is so important. As the examples of our high performers show, even the most talented people fail – particularly when they're in environments that don't suit them. This is not something to be ashamed of – it is what makes us human.

But by identifying where our true strengths lie, we can turn our failures around. We can learn to spot the areas in which we alone excel. And we can turn this excellence into a high performance career – and a high performance life.

LESSON SUMMARY

- Everyone has strengths and everyone has weaknesses. Yet all too often we obsess over the things we can't do, and ignore the things we can.
- Remember the theory of multiple intelligence: there are myriad ways to be talented. The trick is to find yours.
- That involves three steps. First, recognition – think about those instances, perhaps in your youth, when you were told you had a talent. Was it a 'golden seed moment'?
- Second, reflection – think about what you're good at in the here and now. Success leaves clues. It's your job to spot them.
- Third, rhythm – seek out those tasks that induce a sense of 'flow'. These moments are all too rare, but might just reveal your true calling.
- Finding these skills is the quickest route to high performance. Each of us can play to our 'comparative advantage' – provided we know how to find it.

How you are now isn't how you'll always be. How you think now isn't how you'll always think.

LESSON 5

GET FLEXIBLE

'The first day I walked in, I arrived at reception and it wasn't what I wanted it to be. I sat down in reception and there was an old *Daily Mail* on the table from the previous week, and coffee cups that had dried coffee still sitting there.'

Toto Wolff, leader of the world's most successful Formula 1 team, was telling us about his first impressions upon visiting his new headquarters. They weren't great. 'I couldn't believe that this was the Mercedes Formula 1 team,' he laughed. 'This was not what I expected to see.'

Wolff wasn't the type to be relaxed about sloppy standards. With a background in the venture capital industry, in the late 2000s he had made the leap into F1, becoming Williams' executive director in 2012. He soon carved out a reputation for his exacting approach to the sport.

At Mercedes, however, things were even more personal. Not only was he their incoming director of motorsport, he had also acquired a 30 per cent stake in the team, double what he had held at Williams. This time, it wasn't just his reputation on the line – it was his fortune.

It was a shame, then, that Mercedes were underperforming. The German automaker had bought the F1 team for an estimated

$120 million in late 2009 and kept the former management team, led by Ross Brawn, in place. Despite long being one of the sport's greatest principals, in the years that followed Brawn struggled to keep Mercedes' momentum up. In 2010 the team finished fourth, in 2012 fifth.

Wolff had an unusual solution. He believed that much of the problem was down to those coffee cups. 'Now you may say, "How do dry coffee cups or an old *Daily Mail* impact on the performance of a Formula 1 team?", but it shows an attitude, it shows a lack of attention to detail,' he told us.

In that moment, Wolff was offering an unusual solution to a big problem. What if Mercedes' fortunes weren't being undermined by anything as obvious as bad engineering, or the quality of their drivers? What if they were being undermined by thousands of tiny, even unnoticeable factors – starting with those dried-out mugs?

Not many people focus on these 'soft factors', Wolff told us, but actually they are essential: 'All that is part of the values of a team. And if everybody runs in the same direction, if everybody acknowledges that attention to detail is important, then eventually the wheel is going to gain some momentum.'

Over the next few months, Wolff would set about building that momentum. Out went the old *Daily Mail*s and coffee cups; in came a laser-like focus on the minutest features of Mercedes' approach. The results were extraordinary. Within a year of taking over, Mercedes' driver Lewis Hamilton won the title. Over the next few years, Mercedes would become a dominant force in F1, winning the tournament for seven years straight.

There's a lesson here about high performance. Think of the greatest innovations of our time: Thomas Edison working out how to produce light without combustion, Marie Curie discovering radioactivity, the Wright brothers achieving the first powered flight. In each case, the inventors encountered a problem: a world dependent on cumbersome candles and gas lamps; a lack of understanding about how atoms fit together; the irritating fact that birds could fly but humans couldn't. And, in each case, they came up with a creative and audacious solution. Toto Wolff arriving at the Mercedes headquarters represented just such a moment.

These people were problem-solvers. And the way they solved problems was through flexibility – coming up with new ways of approaching an old question. Why should I accept the traditional way of thinking about this issue? What if I developed a completely different method? They show that breakthroughs come from those who are prepared to think and behave differently.

It's harder than it sounds. Most of us possess a fixed model of the world in our head. In the language of psychology, these mental models are known as 'heuristics'. Think of them as 'rules of thumb' – simple problem-solving strategies that allow us to make sense of our surroundings.

These rules can be remarkably useful, especially when we have to reach a correct decision quickly and without all of the information. Consider the question of what to have for breakfast. Instead of starting each day by balancing off all the available info (this cereal is tastier, that one is healthier), you take a shortcut: I ate this yesterday, so I'll eat it again today. It's a simple behavioural hack – one that stops you being overwhelmed by all the information you have to take in every day.

But, while they're generally helpful, these heuristics can undermine our ability to respond to a situation flexibly. They can mean that we get stuck in behavioural grooves that are difficult to get out of.

In the early 1970s, two psychologists, Daniel Kahneman and Amos Tversky, set out to understand how these heuristic shortcuts influence people's behaviour. They suspected that smart people were not particularly methodical or rational, instead making decisions using imperfect mental models. To test this hypothesis, they sent questionnaires to a group of people with high IQs, asking them about areas they knew little about. A truly rational person would set out to analyse the questions methodically from scratch. In fact, most of the respondents fell back on their heuristics – they used rough rules of thumb to explain situations that they barely understood. 'When making judgements under uncertainty, people rely on a limited number of heuristics which sometimes yield reasonable judgements and sometimes lead to severe errors,' they concluded.[1]

Over the next few decades, Kahneman and Tversky would uncover dozens of heuristics – and reveal how they can negatively affect people's decision-making. These 'heuristic biases' lead people to make bad calls. Humans tend to underestimate the amount of time it will take to finish a task. We are more influenced by potential losses than potential gains. We tend to judge the likelihood of events based on how easily we can imagine them – the more 'available' a piece of information is to our minds, the more important it seems. Above all, these mental models can stand in the way of problem-solving. They discourage us from thinking creatively about the behaviours that make up our day-to-day lives – forcing us to get trapped in outmoded ways of doing things. I had Weetabix yesterday, so I'll have it again today.

High performers do things differently. Many know how to smash through their biases. They develop new and creative solutions to their problems. In other words, they have a 'flexible perspective'. This chapter will show how you can get a flexible perspective, too.

HIGH PERFORMANCE PIT STOP –
THE POWER OF FLEXIBILITY

Jake

It was 2007, and I had a problem. For years, I had harboured an ambition to be a sports presenter. To be precise, I wanted to be the best-respected sports presenter in the UK. Unfortunately, this wasn't quite the job I had. As a BBC children's TV host, I spent many days dressed as a giant pink lobster, being directed to pop foam-filled balloons by seven-year-olds. If ever I needed some creative thinking, it was then.

And so I took the initiative. I decided to meet up with someone from the BBC's sports team, and pitch for a sports presenting job. I opened the meeting with my classic stories – failing my A-Levels, getting fired from McDonalds. I thought it made me seem charmingly self-effacing. My colleague disagreed. 'We don't tend to employ people like you,' he said.

Until that moment, I'd thought I was a big deal. Working in children's TV can trick you like that. I was frequently on BBC One, getting stopped in the street to sign autographs, and used to children screaming when they saw me. My conversation with BBC Sport made me realise I wasn't a long way up the TV ladder, I was just a long way up the children's TV ladder.

So I did something drastic. I dropped the BBC's head of football an email, and told him I would do anything to get into sports presenting. This time, I approached things with more humility: I said I would be as flexible as necessary, whatever might get me a step closer to that dream.

He came back with an offer: to do some odd-job reporting on the afternoon football results programme, *Final Score*. That entailed collecting a mic and camera, driving to a third- or fourth-division football match, and dialling into Television Centre to deliver a twenty-second match report. Because these games were in the lower leagues, I would often get bumped from the schedule at the last minute. I'd schlep all the way to, say, Northumberland to not even get on TV.

It wasn't glamorous, but today I think the whole thing was a lesson in the power of creative thinking. After that first conversation with my BBC Sport colleague, I'd thought it was game over – they didn't want people like me. But then I'd begun to wonder what a more creative response would entail. What if there wasn't just one way into sports presenting? What if I could work my way up from the bottom, like I had when I was eighteen?

Sure enough, after a period presenting kids' TV on weekdays and football at weekends, I was given the chance to do some 'proper' sports presenting – and I never looked back. I've come to look back on the experience fondly, lobster costume included. It reminds me of the power of a flexible perspective. When someone tells you something can't be done, ask them 'Why not?' When someone implies you don't have what it takes, ask, 'Then how do I get it?'

HAVE A LITTLE FAITH

'This is it … This. Is. It … Work your arses off.'[2]

These were the instructions barked by Ben Ainslie to the crew of the Oracle team's AC72 catamaran, moments before they ploughed through the finish line forty-four seconds ahead of the runners-up, New Zealand. It was September 2013, and Ainslie had just triumphed in one of the most remarkable finals in the 162-year history of the America's Cup – the most prestigious sailing tournament in the world. Ainslie's victory was the first time a British sailor had been aboard the winning boat since 1903.

'Bugger,' tweeted New Zealand's Prime Minister John Key.[3]

Yet just one week earlier, Team Oracle had been verging on fiasco. 'We were looking down the barrel of a gun,' Oracle's Australian skipper, Jimmy Spithill, would later recall.[4] The team had been demoralised even before the tournament began, starting with a two-point penalty for cheating in the earlier America's Cup world series (they had loaded their boat with illegal weights). From there, things had only got worse. Oracle lost eight of their first eleven races, trailing 8–1 to New Zealand.

The billionaire tech founder Larry Ellison, who was funding the Oracle team, had once declared that he 'hates to lose'. It looked like he was going to have to get used to it. But before he resigned himself to defeat, Ellison had one last throw of the dice. After the fifth race, Ellison replaced the boat's tactician, John Kostecki, with Ainslie, then a four-time Olympic sailing gold medallist.

Soon everything changed. To widespread astonishment, Oracle staged a fierce comeback, winning seven consecutive races, electrifying the contest and setting up the winner-takes-all decider – a decider that, against all odds, Oracle won. 'The Americans were beaten until Ben joined the boat,' recalled Robin Knox-Johnston, the first person to perform a one-man non-stop circumnavigation of the world. 'There's no question it was Ben's arrival which changed the chemistry completely.'[5]

When we met Ainslie for the *High Performance* podcast, we had one question: how did he do it? In his smart first-floor office in Portsmouth, looking across the glistening waters of the Solent,

Ainslie explained his process for building a high performance team. It hadn't come naturally. 'To start off with, if I'm brutally honest, I was rubbish at it,' he told us, harking back to his earliest experience of leadership in the early 2000s. 'I set really high standards for myself, and then you have those expectations of others ... If someone was making a mistake, rather than actually trying to support that person and help them adapt, and grow as a team, quite often I'd just get frustrated.'

So, what is the knack to turning a team around? On one level, the answer is all about a flexible perspective. Ainslie says his skill lay in bringing different approaches together, all to develop something wholly fresh. 'Going into sailing with the Oracle team for 2013, we had a lot of the key people who were from the original team New Zealand that won the [America's] cup in '95,' he said. 'We were marrying that with an American approach to sport – leading to a completely different approach in the end.'

On another level, though, it was all about building up the team's sense of what is possible. Before setting out to solve a group's problem, Ainslie tries to convince them that their problem *could* be solved. 'It's about identifying the issues and also lifting team spirit and bringing a positive belief in our capabilities,' he said in one interview. 'People are down at those moments and you need to keep positivity going while working out your options.'[6] Or, as he put it on the podcast, good coaching is about 'giving people belief that you can do it ... Just having someone saying, *Come on, you can do this.*'

'It's about giving people belief. Just having someone saying, *Come on, you can do this.*' Ben Ainslie

This 'can-do' belief is something Ainslie had learned at a young age. He told us about the aftermath of one race from his childhood, which hadn't gone well. His father, Roddy, who had sailed in the first Whitbread Round the World Race in 1973, asked him what had gone wrong: 'I got back home and my dad, as he was apt to do, asked me how the race went. And I sort of said, "Oh, I was doing really well, but then I was unlucky, and this and that happened, and it was just really unlucky. I finished third or fourth."'

His dad's response was intriguing. 'He paused for a moment and said, "Well, that's really interesting, because I actually happened to watch the race and I saw that you gave up." ... He said, "Look, if you want to really excel in sport and do really, really well ... If you're going to really make it, you've got to give it 100%."'

To say Ainslie took this lesson on board would be an understatement. Over the next couple of decades, Ainslie would become one of the greatest competitive sailors in history. His can-do attitude would bring him a silver medal in the 1996 Olympics in Atlanta, followed by a solo sailing gold in the next four Olympic Games. Between 1993 and 2012 he was a sailing world champion eleven times.

At the point we met Ainslie, he was trying to take a British team to victory in the America's Cup: no mean feat for a tournament that the UK hadn't won since it started in 1851. Throughout the team's headquarters, you can taste the positive attitude that Ainslie emphasises. Nestled in the heart of Portsmouth's old town, Ineos Team UK inhabits a hulking modern building, adorned in a colossal grey Union Jack. Inside, the walls are covered in optimistic quotes. A quote from George Bernard Shaw reads: 'Those who say it can't be done should not interrupt those who are doing it.' The whole approach is about emphasising that any apparent barriers to victory are surmountable. 'The Tour de France eluded us for a long time too,' Ainslie said of his latest endeavour. 'Then Bradley Wiggins cycled into the history books in 2012.'[7]

In emphasising self-belief above all else, Ainslie hints at the first way to get a flexible perspective. Many of us approach our problems as though they are set in stone – if some issue seems hard to solve, it is unsolvable. But Ainslie's emphasis on self-belief hints at another way to smash through these cognitive traps. We must first convince ourselves that a problem *can* be overcome.

This might seem bizarre. Why would merely believing a problem is solvable help us solve it? It might even seem like setting yourself up for failure. But the evidence is clear: self-belief is the first ingredient in problem-solving.

To understand why, we need to turn to one of the most influential psychological concepts of the last four decades, pioneered by Stanford professor Carol Dweck. Here's a quick exercise. Read the following four sentences, and see which of them rings the most true:

1. You are a certain kind of person, and there is not much that can be done to really change that.
2. No matter what kind of person you are, you can always change substantially.
3. You can do things differently, but the important parts of who you are can't really be changed.
4. You can always change basic things about the kind of person you are.[8]

According to Dweck's research, if you agreed with the first and third statements, you're someone with a 'fixed mindset' – you think the way things are is more or less the way things always will be. And if you agreed with the second and fourth, you have a 'growth mindset' – like Ainslie, you have faith in the ability of your circumstances to change, and to change thanks to your behaviour.

Dweck was intrigued by what impact these two mindsets have on people's problem-solving abilities. She once took 330 students aged eleven or twelve and asked them a series of questions about talent – and intelligence in particular. From there, she identified who had a 'fixed' and who had a 'growth' mindset.

Next, the students were given a series of problems. They gradually became more difficult: the first eight didn't require much thought, the next four were much harder. As the children toiled away, a dramatic pattern emerged. When the kids in the fixed mindset group encountered the harder, final puzzles, they soon began to criticise their own abilities. They would say things like 'I guess I am not very smart,' 'I never did have a good memory' or 'I'm no good at things like this.' Their faith in their own ability crumbled in the face of adversity.

The children with the growth mindset had a different response. When they failed, they didn't start self-flagellating. In many cases, they didn't even consider themselves to be failing – they just saw the harder puzzles as an exciting challenge. In the end, these individuals performed much better than their fixed-mindset peers.

This difference was not just dramatic; it was remarkable. The gap in performance had nothing to do with genetics, intelligence or motivation. Instead, it was down to the difference between mindsets. A growth mindset transforms what is possible.

The moral is clear: if you convince yourself you *can* solve a problem, then you're much more likely to be able to. How you are now isn't how you'll always be. How you think now isn't how you'll always think. We can all change – in fact, being able to change is what makes us human. As Dweck puts it: 'In the growth mindset, you don't feel the need to convince yourself and others that you have a royal flush when you are secretly worried it's a pair of tens. The hand you're dealt is just the starting point.'[9]

This insight has profound implications for our lives. It suggests that, if we want to overcome some difficulty, we first need to boost our sense of what is achievable. Think of Ben Ainslie, with his string of apparently hopeless goals, first taking on saving the Oracle team, next embarking on winning the America's Cup for the UK. The problem seems insurmountable – but that just makes it a compelling challenge.

Of course, it's one thing to admire people with a growth mindset, and quite another to actually learn from them. Changing one's mindset is no mean feat – it involves a fundamental rewiring of how you approach problems. But Dweck's research is clear. A growth mindset isn't just something you're born with. It's something you can acquire.

How? Well, one of the most compelling tools Dweck offers is a simple reframing of our problems. She suggests we can boost our sense of the possible by simply adding three letters to our sentences – the word 'yet'.

Many of us, after trying something new and challenging, love to declare that we're no good at it. We quickly pass a judgement with a firm sense of finality: 'I can't solve that puzzle.' 'I don't know how to pass this exam.' 'I can't deal with this problem.' It's a little like the dogs we met in Lesson 1, who refused to leave their electrified cage. We see a temporary problem, and label it a permanent one.

But there's an alternative. Whenever you find yourself thinking a problem is insurmountable, try adding the word 'yet'. It's a small change, but a powerful one. 'I can't solve that puzzle *yet*'.

'I don't know how to pass this exam *yet*.' 'I can't deal with this problem *yet*.'

This small change, Dweck's research shows, can fundamentally rewire how we think about the obstacles we face. The addition of 'yet' subtly tweaks our mindset – making us more optimistic about our ability to change. 'Just the words "yet" or "not yet",' she says, gives people 'greater confidence, and a path to the future that creates greater persistence.'[10]

It's an outlook Ben Ainslie would recognise. In February 2021, Ineos Team UK fell at one of the last hurdles in their attempt to make it into the America's Cup – being beaten by the Italian team Luna Rossa in the penultimate round. But within weeks, Ainslie was back in Portsmouth, preparing for his next challenge.

At the time of writing, Britain still hasn't won the America's Cup. Yet.

HIGH PERFORMANCE PIT STOP:
CRISIS REIMAGINED

One useful tool for developing a growth mindset is inspired by Marcelino Sambé – principal dancer of the Royal Ballet.

Sambé had none of the privileges that usually define ballet dancers' childhoods. He first discovered his love of dance at a community centre for children with troubled families on the outskirts of Lisbon. Against the odds, Sambé would win a place at the National Conservatory in Lisbon – despite going to his audition in a tracksuit, and the fact he 'didn't know what ballet was'. A few years later, he would join the Royal Ballet Upper School in London, becoming first a soloist and then a principal dancer.

But his lesson in the power of a growth mindset came after a major setback. He got a deep stress fracture in his shin. It wasn't fun. 'Getting injured is terrible because you know you're going to have so much work to come back,' he told us. And his particular injury was the worst of all: 'A stress fracture is so bad for a ballet dancer because it's the springs: imagine a spring that is broken.' His physio's advice was clear: no jumping.

When Sambé came on the podcast, we were intrigued by how he managed to overcome this injury. His great skill was reframing his injury not as a setback, but as an opportunity. It gave him a chance to try different experiences – ones he had missed out on due to his focus on his career. 'I did a lot of reading, studying,' he told us. 'A lot of exciting things that could further me as a person as well as as a dancer ... I was like, "What do I like? What do I want? OK, let's look at art." I went to all the museums. Hung out with lots of drag queens, and other super-exciting people around London.'

A few years on, and Sambé doesn't quite remember the injury fondly – but he recognises that it taught him something. 'It really fed my excitement to come back with a new perspective of things,' he said. 'Those nine months were pivotal for my career and pivotal for me ... I feel like if I hadn't gone through that nine months of really understanding who I am and asking, "What do I want? What do I really want?" I would have not looked at the director and have him go, "He's ready."' The injury had made him the best dancer he could be.

There's a powerful lesson here. Think about a setback you've experienced in your own life – a problem at work, perhaps. Next, write down two positive ways in which your behaviour changed as a result. Did you learn a valuable insight into how your company works? Did it teach you to be more resilient? Like Sambé, we can all reframe our problems as chances to get a new perspective – we just need the right mindset.

THINK LIKE A MAD SCIENTIST

A growth mindset might be enough to convince you that you *can* solve a problem. But it doesn't offer much insight into *how*. For more practical insights into the art of problem-solving, we need to turn elsewhere – and a good place to start is the research of the psychologist Karl Duncker.

Born in 1903 in Germany, from early in his life Duncker became obsessed with the way people think about objects. His argument was simple: once we have started to think of an object as doing one thing, it becomes almost impossible to imagine it doing another thing.

Take Duncker's most famous experiment. He gave a group of students a box of pins, a candle and a matchbook – and told them to find a way to attach the candle to the wall. They were stumped. Some of them attempted to melt the candle to the wall; others experimented with pushing the drawing pins through the wax into the wall, with little success.

In fact, there was a simple way to solve the problem: tack the box to the wall and put the candle inside it. But very few of the participants thought to do so. Why?

Duncker thought the answer lay in what he called 'functional fixedness'. When we see an object, we become fixated on its main function – in this case, the box was holding pins, and so nobody thought that it could hold a candle. This limits our ability to think critically about what is possible.[11]

Functional fixedness is not limited to boxes and candles. The term refers to the myriad ways our problem-solving can get stuck: we become wedded to one way of resolving an issue, and can't imagine any alternatives.

Imagine, for example, you have six glasses of orange juice. The first three glasses are full; the next three are empty. The game is that you have to move the glasses so that the full and empty ones alternate. But, there's a catch: you can only move one glass. Can you do it?

For most people, this problem seems insurmountable. Many try to move the second full glass to sit in between two empty glasses, only to realise that this still leaves two full glasses next to each other. But there is a way: pour the juice from the second glass into the second-to-last glass, then put the second glass back in its original place.

Did you struggle to solve this problem? That's functional fixedness. In your head, you only imagined changing the glasses' places – you weren't flexible enough to imagine pouring the orange juice.

Or consider the following. Let's say you have baked a beautiful chocolate cake that you want to divide into eight equal pieces. The snag is that the knife you are using is unreliable – it will snap after you use it just three times. How do you slice the cake into eight equal pieces with just three cuts?

If you're like most people, you probably first cut the cake in half vertically, then you'll cut it in half horizontally. Then you'll start making a third cut diagonally, before realising that this only makes six slices of cake, not all the same size. So, what do you do? You might start plotting to cut some irregular looking cake slices, but remember, the rule is that all the pieces have to be equal.

There is a simple answer, though. Go ahead and make the first two cuts, creating four slices of cake. Then then look at the cake from the side on – and cut it all the way through. Voilà.[12]

Did this one bamboozle you too? That's functional fixed-ness: in your head, you only imagined the cake from above. You weren't flexible enough to see it from the side.

You might be thinking: what does any of this have to do with high performance? Surprisingly, the answer is: quite a lot. This fixed approach is exactly how we confront the issues in our daily lives – when we get stuck at work, or when we run into trouble in our relationships. We get trapped in a particular way of doing things, and lose sight of the alternative, more creative solutions.

But functional fixedness can be overcome. In all of the above cases, the solution is to change your perspective (in the case of the cake, quite literally). And that's how we should respond to the problems we face in life, too.

Imagine how a mad scientist would respond to the problems identified above. They wouldn't be hampered by their pre-existing assumptions about how to cut a cake, or how to arrange their orange juice. In each case, they would see past what *is* to imagine what *could be*. They view the challenge afresh, unburdened by any heuristic traps.

This is our second tool for getting a flexible perspective: every time you encounter a problem, try to see it as if for the first time. We call this mad-scientist thinking.

Easy to say, you might think. But how can we all learn to develop this kind of fresh perspective? An illustrative example comes from the example of Leicester City. In 2015, Leicester had a big problem: they just weren't that good at football. (Well, to be fair, they weren't that good by Premier League standards.) At the start of the 2015–16 season, the club were given odds of 5000/1 to finish as champions.

The season before, they had narrowly avoided relegation from the Premier League and subsequently sacked Nigel Pearson, the head coach. They replaced him with Claudio Ranieri, the veteran

Italian manager who had only recently been sacked as manager of the Greek national team, following a disastrous four months at the helm. The appointment made Leicester one of the book-maker's favourites for relegation. It didn't help that they were running low on funds. In *Soccernomics*, the economist Stefan Szymanski and the journalist Simon Kuper wrote that money determines 80–90 per cent of the performance of football clubs.[13] In 2014–15, Leicester spent the third lowest amount – £57 million – in wages for the season. (The biggest-spending club, Chelsea, spent £217 million.)

And then the script changed. In 2015–16, Leicester seemed to defy gravity. The club won a series of stunning victories against some of the greatest – and most valuable – teams in the world. For the first time in Leicester's history, they won the league. Five years later, they would defy the odds again to win the FA cup. Leicester had solved their problem in the most dramatic way imaginable.

There's one player whose career seems to represent Leicester's astonishing turnaround better than anyone: Kasper Schmeichel, the Danish international goalkeeper. Schmeichel was an integral part of Leicester's expectation-busting run in 2015–16.

But things weren't always going so well for the player. A decade previously, Schmeichel had started his career at Manchester City. He soon felt he was stagnating. He was being given too few oppor-tunities to establish himself, and was often being sent out on loan to lower-league clubs like Darlington, Falkirk and Bury. He felt demoralised. The son of one of the greatest goalkeepers in modern history, Manchester United's Peter Schmeichel, Kasper knew he had more in him – but somehow he couldn't get up to scratch.

And so Schmeichel did something drastic: he reset his career. After several seasons of drifting from club to club, Schmeichel made the dramatic decision to 'restart' his professional life by moving down three divisions to play for Notts County. 'It was kind of like trying to get your WiFi to work and it won't,' he told us. 'You keep resetting it, keep resetting it and it doesn't work in the end. You have to turn off the computer and restart. It was the same thing for me. I had to restart my career.'

'If you don't believe it yourself, no one else is going to believe you.'
Kasper Schmeichel

This change was just what Schmeichel needed. While at Notts County, he had a powerful conversation with his father, Peter, who taught him how to make the most of his professional restart. 'I had harboured a secret ambition of wanting to win the Premier League but I was reluctant to share this outside of my own inner circle,' he recalled. His father challenged him, Kasper told us. '"If you are going to believe it, you should commit to it and tell people,"' his father said.

Kasper seized the opportunity – deciding that he was going to announce his goal in public. 'I was due to give a speech back at my old school and I decided that was the place where I was going to go public on my ambition for the first time,' he said. 'I reasoned, the ability to convince yourself of something is so important because, if you don't believe it yourself, no one else is going to believe you.'

It's worth slowing down to take a look at this method. Arguably, Schmeichel's problem was that he had fallen into a heuristic bias – developing a fixed sense of his abilities, and thinking that he could never be the person he wanted to. And so, to transform his behaviour, he decided to start again.

Sure enough, telling the pupils and teachers at his alma mater lit a flame in Schmeichel. 'I started to push myself to be the best,' he told us. 'I wanted to prove I was the best.' From there, as if by magic, Schmeichel came to regain his self-belief – and his form. In 2011, Sven-Göran Eriksson – under whom Schmeichel had served at Manchester City and Notts County – signed him for Leicester, who were languishing in the Championship. Nearly 400 appearances later and Schmeichel is viewed as one of his generation's leading goalkeepers. When, on 2 May 2016, Leicester lifted the league cup for the first time, his great reset came to fruition. 'I didn't prove anyone wrong. I proved myself right,' he told us.

There's a lesson here for all of us. Schmeichel's professional restart hinted at how we can all use creativity to get out of a rut. Imagine what a reset would look like in your life. Imagine thinking like a mad scientist.

THE YIN-YANG PRINCIPLE

'I always liken starting a business to being a parent. And so when I had my firstborn business, just like a child, there was no way that that was going anywhere but up. I was never going to let it down.'

Holly Tucker's enthusiasm for her business in infectious. Even via a grainy Zoom video, she managed to excite us with her boundless passion for business – recounting how she built an award-winning, multimillion pound company. Founded from her kitchen table, Not On The High Street is today worth millions – and has pumped £1 billion into the small business community. Customers visit to buy all manner of personalised gifts – from hand-crafted jewellery to wooden tools.

But it wasn't always easy. 'When I was twenty-three, I was diagnosed with a brain tumour. After the initial shock and discovery that it was benign, my first marriage was also on the rocks,' she told us. At the time, Tucker was running a small business, but that soon fell through: 'I put on weight and the start-up business I had begun, a bridal website, came to an end. It was a tough time and I was at a low ebb. I was forced to go back to my initial job of consulting in advertising sales.'

Tucker's experience offers another lesson in how we can let our problems overwhelm us. Something unfortunate happens, and we encounter a setback. From there, it can feel almost impossible to get back on to our feet.

Except that isn't how it panned out for Tucker. It started with her notebook. 'I had always carried around a purple notebook in which I would jot down all my creative ideas,' she told us. 'There was no pattern to them, I would write whatever random idea came to mind.'

From these jottings, the idea for Not On The High Street was born. It began with Tucker's desire to create something for herself: 'I wanted to be creative and to scratch this itch, so I designed some Christmas wreaths made out of usual things, such as chillies, oranges and cinnamon sticks. I had a vague plan to sell them at craft fairs during the weekends.'

In the process, Tucker spotted a gap in the market. 'I assumed there would be one near my home. There wasn't, so I set one up with a loan from my Dad,' she recalled. From the first time she held that fair – at which anyone could come and sell their craft goods – she realised she was on to something good. 'We held the first fair in Chiswick and the atmosphere was buzzing,' she told us. 'That was when I had my lightbulb moment.'

Tucker discovered that most of the fair's vendors had a problem: they had nowhere to sell their goods. 'These creative, talented producers of quirky, handmade, clever and beautiful objects were frustrated,' she told us. 'They knew people wanted to buy their stuff ... but it was hard to let anyone know where they were.' As a result, many of them were trapped selling things from their houses – with limited success: 'They could hardly rely on passing trade. For the most part, they had to sell to friends or to one or two local shops and hope that word of mouth would get them more customers.'

'That was where I could come in,' Tucker said. Her idea was simple: to create an online marketplace for thousands of independent sellers, providing technology, business advice and marketing. And so Not On The High Street was born. Today, the company offers millions of original items from hundreds of creative small businesses – bespoke homeware, jewellery, wedding accessories, you name it.

How does Tucker account for the success of her business? The answer hints at our third key lesson on problem-solving. Like Schmeichel, on one level Tucker's success lies in her ability to see her problems from a wholly fresh perspective. 'My naivety was my greatest strength,' Holly observed. 'I didn't know what had been tried, what worked and what was or wasn't possible. This was my superpower.'

But Tucker emphasises that it wasn't just her naivety that led to her business's rapid growth – it was the way that naivety was complemented by the very different mindset of a colleague. Early in the company's story, Tucker had teamed up with Sophie Cornish, who became her co-founder and business partner. Their mutually beneficial outlooks would become key to the company's growth. As Tucker explained to us:

We have balance and an ability to appreciate both sides of the brain. I am the one who will take an idea and run farthest with it. I'm the one who builds up to an ambitious financial forecast that spells out the thrilling success. Sophie would put together the business plan. This involves doing the heavy-duty research, understanding the market, the customers, the realities and thrashing out the detail.

Put simply, one of them focused on the future, the other on the present. Tucker has suggested that this approach is much like the ancient Chinese theory of yin and yang: 'I've found that if you try to strive to find people who can accept their strong and weaker points, who are happy to work in a yin-yang way with others, and complement them – this is a winning type of DNA.'[14] Her company's success was the result of two different heuristics – one planning ahead, one focusing on the here and now.

 'Find people who can accept their strong and weaker points, who are happy to work in a yin-yang way with others.' Holly Tucker

Many organisational psychologists would agree. Getting a wide array of viewpoints around a table, they say, can boost everyone's performance. The argument can be distilled down to a simple insight: great minds think differently. In psychology, this breadth of different worldviews is known as 'cognitive diversity'. Teams that are more cognitively diverse have a wider array of opinions. They see all the most important questions in different ways. Often, when they first start tackling a problem, they agree on very little.

You might think that this is a recipe for disaster. If you can't agree on anything, how can you solve a problem? But the science indicates the opposite. In one study from the *Harvard Business Review*, two academics analysed the performance of 100 different groups in a variety of different settings. What they found shocked them. Almost without fail, the wider the array of views, the better the performance. As the article's title summarised it, 'Teams solve problems faster when they're more cognitively diverse'.[15]

How can this be so? Well, according to the academics, it's a numbers game. The more opinions you have, the more likely you are to stumble upon one that solves the problem. You might have a blind spot, but someone who's wildly different might not share it. Think of Tucker, with her creative mind but her D ('Or was it an E?') in business studies, and Sophie Cornish, with her archly analytical mind. As Tucker put it, 'It's the way Not On The High Street was born: two women who, in those early years, were seeing both sides of the coin.'[16] Next time you're facing a thorny problem, don't tackle it alone – try to find someone who's the yin to your yang.

GREAT MINDS THINK DIFFERENTLY

Toto Wolff had some words of warning for anyone interested in high performance: 'The most dangerous phrase in the language of a high performer is "We've always done it this way."'

 'The most dangerous phrase in the language of a high performer is "We've always done it this way."' Toto Wolff

Wolff should know. When he arrived at Mercedes, not everyone believed in his strategy. For one thing, he was replacing one of the greatest visionaries in the sport's history, Ross Brawn – the man who led Michael Schumacher to seven world championship titles. And for another, he wasn't even an experienced F1 team leader – his background was in venture capital.

Yet Wolff proved everyone wrong. And he did so by breaking the mould.

Wolff's story is surprisingly common. This book is filled with people with an unusual perspective – and who used that perspective to shake things up. Think of Jo Malone building a perfume empire without being able to memorise a formulation, or Zack George transforming from massively overweight teenager to CrossFit champion in just a couple of years.

It's tempting to think that these high performers triumphed in spite of the odds – that Malone became a world-leading perfumer *even though* she had no formal training, or that George became a champion *in spite of* his earlier lack of drive.

But this chapter hints at the opposite interpretation. It's tempting to think that high performers triumphed despite the odds. But what if these people succeeded not in spite of, but *because of*, their unusual experiences?

We've seen that when it comes to solving a hard problem, the worst thing to do is fall back on the obvious, tried-and-tested solution. It's a recipe for falling into heuristic traps, getting stuck in your old ways of doing things, unable to see the big picture.

The best way to actually overcome our problems is to see them anew – to develop a fresh perspective. If Ben Ainslie hadn't had an idiosyncratic outlook, he would never have believed it possible to take Oracle to victory. If Kasper Schmeichel hadn't hit reset on his career, he would never have become one of the country's best goalkeepers. If Holly Tucker had had the typical businessperson's background, with an MBA and an obsessively analytical focus, she would never have had the vision to build Not On The High Street.

All of these stories hint at a wholly new way of solving our thorniest problems. If you find yourself getting stuck, the worst response is to go with the crowd. Great minds rarely think alike. Great minds think differently.

LESSON SUMMARY

- When we encounter problems, we often use tried-and-tested shortcuts to solve them. These 'heuristics' can be useful, but also stop us being creative.
- Effective problem-solving is all about smashing through your heuristics – and gaining a flexible perspective.
- How can we learn to think flexibly? First, convince yourself that the puzzles you encounter *can* be solved. It's not that you can't do it – it's that you can't do it *yet*.
- Second, learn to look at things afresh. Try thinking like a mad scientist. If you were encountering this problem without any preconceptions, what would you do?
- Third, get outside yourself. Ask the opinion of someone completely unlike you – do they have a different take?
- Above all, remember that seeing things in an unusual way isn't the problem – it's the solution. High performers do things differently.

Talent might be the spark of high performance. But habits are what keep the fire burning.

FIND YOUR NON-NEGOTIABLES

I n 1997, England's rugby team was ranked sixth in the world. Things felt stale. Despite lots of able players, the team hadn't improved a jot in over a decade. In one study, conducted by Loughborough University, rugby players were ranked as the fifteenth fittest sportsmen in the country – coming in behind archers.[1]

And yet within six years, England would be lifting the Webb Ellis cup, the culmination of a tournament in which they proved themselves to be the best rugby team in the world. What had changed?

The short answer: Clive Woodward.

Woodward, who was appointed manager in 1997, was no ordinary coach. This was the man who had previously taken the provincial club Henley from regional irrelevance into the national leagues, claiming a series of stunning tournament victories along the way. The man who had brought the embattled team London Irish back from the brink of insolvency. And the man who had achieved all of this while rugby was still an amateur sport – meaning that elite, international players would have to balance the demands of the game alongside their 'proper' jobs.

Sure enough, Woodward's coaching was transformative. The England Woodward took to victory in the 2003 world cup were unrecognisable from the team of just six years previously.

How did Woodward do it? At first glance, his toolkit seemed varied – ranging from a tireless work ethic and forensic attention to detail, to an unrivalled ability to learn from disciplines beyond sport. But, upon closer inspection, players began to realise that Woodward's power could be summarised with one word: consistency.

At first, this wasn't obvious to us. When we sat down in Woodward's perfectly manicured garden and asked him to explain how he got the best out of his players, he responded unexpectedly: 'How do you define time?'

There was a pause. Your two authors looked at each other, perplexed. But, after a moment, Woodward explained. This was the question he had posed to the England squad in an early training session. It was not quite as profound as it sounded:

> I was not interested in [England's World Cup-winning captain] Martin Johnson's views on ancient philosophy. As intelligent as he is, I don't believe he has strong views on the concept of time. What I did know was that unless we, as a team, could agree on how we would define time – and most importantly, the rules around punctuality and how we would operate – then we would not work as cohesively, ergonomically or efficiently as we should.

A consistent approach to time, Woodward said, was crucial. 'I started with time deliberately as I believe it says more about a person or a group than anything else. How can you work with someone who does not understand and appreciate the importance of time?'

Woodward emphasised that this approach is not about having an obsession with rules. 'I ran away from my naval boarding school because I hated the strict rules. I wasn't empowered, or listened to or involved in any sense. I felt no loyalty, no sense of belonging,' he said. But when it comes to building high perform-ance behaviour, it's crucial to agree a collection of unnegotiable behaviours. 'These were the rules we would all consistently live by,' Woodward told us.

In his book *Winning!*, Woodward describes how his team of world-beating players including Johnson, Lawrence Dallaglio and Jason Leonard took the message on board. They came to talk about 'Lombardi time', which meant that the team would be fifteen minutes early to all appointments involving the England team. The term 'Lombardi time' is named for Vince Lombardi, who coached the Wisconsin-based Green Bay Packers in the 1960s. In Lombardi's words: 'Winning isn't a some-time thing; it's an all-time thing. You don't win once in a while; you don't do things right once in a while; you do them right all of the time.'[2]

This is why consistent behaviour is so crucial. 'Consistent habits like timekeeping set standards of behaviour, and slipping standards have an insidious impact on performance,' Woodward wrote. 'Discipline with timekeeping is non-negotiable. This was a tiny but essential moment in our evolution as a winning culture.'[3]

'It's about consistency of performance. Are they playing day in, week in, week out?' Tracey Neville

That's why the sixth principle of high performance is one Woodward would support: consistency. So far in this book, we've learned how high performers take responsibility for their actions and motivate themselves, and we've touched on how they play to their strengths and act creatively. But all of this is useless if they can't maintain it in the long run.

Tracey Neville, former head coach of the England Roses netball team, once told us about the power of consistency in distinguishing a good club player from a national-level one. 'A lot of players think if they're fit, that means they can come and play a [world cup] tournament. Well, no. It's about consistency of performance,' she said. 'Are they playing day in, week in, week out? Players that are not are going to be no good at world cup.'

It was a powerful lesson on the power of consistency. It's consistency that turns one-time high performers into all-time high performers. It's consistency that turns a group of skilled but undisciplined sportspeople into a world cup-winning team. And it's consistency that lets you excel for a lifetime, not just a moment. If you want to master high performance, consistency is everything.

TRADEMARK BEHAVIOURS

Once we started asking our high performers about consistency, we discovered that almost all of them thought it was essential. We started to notice, for example, that Lombardi time wasn't limited to the England Rugby team. Almost all of our high performers would arrive early for the interview – and told us timekeeping was an area in which they wouldn't compromise.

Take Chris Hoy. Before we met him, we were worried that he would struggle to find the spot – the room we had secured for the interview was hidden away in a backstreet of Manchester's Northern Quarter. On the cold, rainy December morning we were due to meet with him, a strong umbrella, Google Maps and lots of patience were necessary. But we needn't have worried. At ten to ten, there was a gentle tap on the door. Standing outside was Britain's greatest-ever Olympian. We thanked Chris for his timely arrival. 'Of course,' he nonchalantly replied. 'I hate arriving anywhere late. I am always on time.'

At another interview, Tracey Neville told us the same thing: 'I hate being late.' So too did Sean Dyche, the manager of Burnley FC: 'Turn up on time. Every time. No problem.'

After a while, we came up with a term for these consistent, non-negotiable habits – 'trademark behaviours'. A trademark behaviour is one that you commit to unequivocally. When a situation gets tough and everything else disintegrates, these trademark behaviours remain in place. Your commitment to these behaviours, through thick and thin, makes for high performance. 'You want to perform well? Then commit,' was how Steven Gerrard put it to us.

'You want to perform well? Then commit.' Steven Gerrard

In high performance environments, those who fail to live up to their trademark behaviours tend to come under fire. One particularly telling example comes from the memoir of Roy Keane, the number two to Alex Ferguson at Manchester United in the 2000s – and a man ever-vigilant for the need for consistency. In his autobiography, Keane recounted an anecdote about Mark Bosnich, an affable Australian goalkeeper, who had been brought in to replace Peter Schmeichel after he left the club in 1999.

Bosnich had arrived an hour late for his first day's training. 'I asked him where he had been,' Keane wrote. '"I got lost on the way from the hotel," he smirked. He was a bit of a smirker. "Get fucking lost," I sneered ... "Your first fucking day at Manchester United and you turn up an hour late for fucking training,"' Keane said.[4] He described how he too had once been put up in the hotel Bosnich was staying in, six years previously, but he had turned up for training an hour early, mindful of the importance of a commitment to timeliness.

But timekeeping isn't the only non-negotiable. On the podcast, Phil Neville recalled playing under Alex Ferguson at Manchester United. Ferguson, he said, emphasised a consistent commitment to small habits – things like dress. 'Sir Alex Ferguson was an absolute stickler,' he told us. 'No jeans on the way to training.' The reason? That this small trademark behaviour – dressing smartly – led to bigger and more important characteristics, such as self-respect and professionalism. 'The minute you walk into the training ground, you look and behave like a Manchester United footballer,' Neville said of Ferguson's outlook. 'Everyone wore a shirt and tie. That's why Manchester United wear blazers, because it was that attention to the simple things.'

Such an approach to tiny, non-negotiable habits might seem irrelevant – even petty. But the science is clear: trademark behaviours are a key ingredient in high performance. In fact, the ability to build consistent behaviours is more important than any other objectives we might set.

In one intriguing study, researchers set out to explore what made for a high-performing organisation. They studied six companies, with a particular focus on what made teams perform at a high level. What, they wondered, did the best organisations have in common?

At first, their results were a mess. In fact, all the groups – good and bad – seemed fairly similar. Most notably, most of the teams had identified a set of clear goals: 89 per cent of the top teams across each company and 86 per cent of the bottom third. Thinking strategically alone wasn't a route to success, then.

But then it clicked. The high-performing groups *did* do things differently, the researchers realised. Their approach to goal-setting was distinct from the others. Instead of goals related to outcomes – hitting a sales target or winning over a client – they set goals related to behaviours, like turning up on time or dressing smartly. If a team aimed to exhibit a consistent set of behaviours, it was significantly more likely to perform well. The discrepancy was striking: 89 per cent of the top third of teams set behavioural goals versus only 33 per cent of the bottom third of teams.[5] Non-negotiables, the study concluded, are the route to excellence.

Many of our high performers got this intuitively. Trademark behaviours are the route to success. As Shaun Wane, head coach of the English rugby league team, put it: 'The only way to win is through consistency. Consistent messages, consistent behaviours and consistent consequences.'

HIGH PERFORMANCE PIT STOP – SECOND-HALF THINKING

In his book *How To Win*, Clive Woodward shared one of the trademark behaviours he used to focus the minds of his team.[6] At half-time in every match, he would ask players to give all their attention to a simple ritual that involved putting on a new kit and thinking about what was going well (and what was going badly). The routine was simple:

0–2 minutes
Absolute silence
Think about performance
New kit

2–5 minutes
Coaches' assessments
Take on food and fluids

5–8 minutes
Coach's final word

8–10 minutes
Absolute silence
Visualise kick-off

Woodward viewed this ritual as a crucial way to get into the right mindset at half-time – it was a non-negotiable.

You can use Woodward's second-half thinking method in your own life. Try to think of the natural breaks that come in your day – when you get up from your desk to get a coffee, for example. Is there a way to use this time constructively by developing a similar ritual? What are the things that you need to focus on in the day ahead – can you list them? Try filling in the gaps:

1–2 minutes
Behaviour:

2–3 minutes
Behaviour:

3–4 minutes
Behaviour:

LEARN YOUR TRADEMARKS

Of all of our high performance interviewees, Shaun Wane had the hardest start in life. Throughout his childhood, Wane's father frequently meted out brutal punishments that left him wishing he were dead. His schoolteachers rarely got to see him – and when they did, his behaviour was terrible. 'I don't have any good memories, I only have bad memories,' Wane told us of his childhood.

Everything came to a head when he was fifteen. After years of escalating misbehaviour, Wane rang in a bomb scare to his school. He was caught almost immediately. 'I went home and my dad nearly killed me,' he would later recount. 'I thought "I'm really going to die here, so I need to get out". I went out, I left my house, I had a ripped t-shirt and no shoes on and I never went back. I had nowhere to go.'[7]

So, when we welcomed Wane on to the podcast, we were intrigued by how he became a high performer. For many people, such a start in life would have been insurmountable – nobody could have blamed Wane if he had never recovered. And yet, somehow, Wane had gone on to become a well-respected player – and then one of greatest coaches in recent rugby league history.

Through the 1980s and early 1990s, Wane played 149 games for the all-conquering Wigan Warriors, and represented Great Britain twice. After eight years' service for Wigan, he was brusquely informed that his time at the club was at an end. It was an unpleasant moment. 'I didn't have a clue,' he told us. 'I wasn't once told where to improve or why they might be thinking of replacing me.' But Wane was only just getting started. He continued his career at Leeds, before eventually returning to his boyhood club, first as a scout and then a junior coach. Upon being given the chance to lead Warriors, he took them to Super League grand final wins in 2013, 2016 and 2018. From 2011–18, he was the most decorated coach in the sport's history. And in 2020, he was appointed head coach of the England team.

How had he turned his life around? Wane puts it down to a few forces. For one thing, there was his childhood sweetheart – and now wife – Lorraine. 'She's had an influence on me,' he told us, with characteristic understatement. When Wane left home, it was Lorraine's parents who took him in. 'This change, meeting Lorraine and moving in with her parents, was the real start of my life. It helped make me a good dad and a good coach,' he said.

For another, there was his determination – above all, his determination not to be anything like his father. 'I remember lying in bed at eight, nine, ten, wishing I was dead. And I thought, *if ever I have kids they're never going to feel this way.*' We asked Wane whether his compassion as a coach was a reaction against his abusive dad. 'It could be,' he told us. 'I'm very passionate about being straight with people ... and I'm very, very passionate about players having a good laugh when [the training's] finished.'

But we were most intrigued by Wane's emphasis on trademark behaviours. Perhaps more than any other high performance interviewee, Wane put his success down to simple, repeated, consistent behaviours. They are what had turned him into a great player, a world-beating coach, and, above all, a better man than his father. 'There's a few principles which I won't bend on,' Wane told us of his coaching style. 'It's non-negotiable: your behaviours, your standards, and the detail of how you're playing.'

In this, Wane was just like the other high performers we'd met. But Wane didn't just talk about these non-negotiables in the abstract. Reading between the lines, we could see that he had developed an unusually clear set of criteria for working out what your non-negotiables should be. And so we can all use Wane's method to find our own trademark behaviours.

The first principle was the most straightforward: *make them simple.* Too many individuals and teams aiming for high performance, Wane suggested, get worked up about irrelevant, even frivolous, details. 'They want bells and whistles, a flashy performance,' he said. But this is a dangerous strategy. If you want to be a high performer, you need to focus on the most basic building blocks of success. 'What I have learned over the years is the stronger the organisation, the better they do the real simple, basic things,' he told us.

'The stronger the organisation, the better they do the real simple, basic things.' Shaun Wane

Like what? we asked. 'For a rugby team, it's your core skills – your catch, your pass, your contact. But it's those real simple basics … For England, I want them doing simple things really, really well.' This is an approach we can all learn from. If you were to distil your chosen field down to its most basic components, what would you get? Once you've stripped out all the grand strategy and abstract theory, many professions can be reduced to a handful of core habits. For a live TV presenter, it's knowing how to keep to a schedule; for a coach, it's about maintaining discipline. What would the equivalent be in your life?

The second principle of a good trademark behaviour was similarly elegant: *make them count*. And in particular, make them count under pressure. Wane suggested that the most important behaviours are those that matter in the most intense moments. We can work out our trademark behaviours by asking: When the going gets tough, what is going to make the difference? He pointed to high-stakes matches lost because players cracked under the stress – and forgot the most basic elements of their sport. 'You look at games, test matches, world cup finals, where teams would turn the ball over – they're simple core skill errors. So don't tell me it's not important,' he told us.

When the pressure is on, everything but the essential behaviours go out of the window. The trick, then, is to work out what trademark behaviours will make a difference in these moments. Imagine a stressful situation in your life: a big pitch meeting, a job interview, even a first date. What behaviours are going to make the difference between success and failure? Your posture? Your tone of voice? Try to work out what matters when the heat is on, and practise it obsessively when the heat is off.

Finally, Wane emphasised the need for the behaviours to be as explicit as possible: in short, *make them clear*. All too often, Wane suggested, teams get derailed by identifying vague and wishy-washy behaviours. Have you ever worked for a company where the CEO is fond of vague, corporate waffle – all 'synergy', 'intentionality' and 'blue-skies thinking'? Wane took the opposite approach. You need your behavioural goals to be unambiguous. When we asked him how he instituted high performance in the teams he said, 'I find that quite easy. Being very, very clear on what you expect.' Trademark behaviours are all about clarity.

But how? The trick, Wane suggests, is to explicitly say – and repeat – the key behaviours you're looking for. 'Tell everybody everything – all the information,' he said. 'You make sure the players understand about your standards and behaviours off the field, and the same when you play.' This is as true for an individual as it is for a team. When you know your own standards inside out, you're more likely to commit to them. Make your trademark behaviours explicit – try writing them down, and pinning them to the wall above your bed or your desk. Your trademark behaviours should constantly be at the forefront of your mind. They are the simple, crucial, clear rules for what you do – and who you are.

_____

TRIGGER POINTS

There's a big difference between identifying a behaviour and actually committing to it, though. And that's where habits come in. Talent might be the spark of high performance. But habits are what keep the fire burning.

Habits are the repeated actions that you do without thinking. You probably have lots of habits you're aware of: brushing your teeth, having dinner at 7:00pm, kissing your children goodnight. You'll also have habits you don't even notice. If you always greet the bus driver on your commute to work, that's a habit. If whenever you walk past the kettle at work you stop for a cup of tea, that's a habit. Habits are everywhere.

The value of habits lies in the fact they happen automatically – you're still in control, but on autopilot. This is the end goal with any trademark behaviour. As Shaun Wane emphasised, the first step to building non-negotiables is making your standards clear, and keeping them at the forefront of your mind; eventually, however, these standards should become so ingrained that you do them without thinking.

How can we build this kind of unthinking adherence to a behaviour? To begin with, we need to understand what is going on when we fall into (or out of) a habit. Charles Duhigg, the author of the bestselling *The Power of Habit*, argues that the science of habits is simple. It's a loop made up of cue, routine and reward.[8]

Say you are working at home. Every afternoon at 2:30pm, you pop down to the kitchen to get a biscuit. This pattern of behaviour soon starts to show on your waistline. What is going on? Well, according to Duhigg, there are three steps. There's the cue: you spot that it's 2:30pm, or you start feeling hungry in the afternoon. There's the routine: you wander into the kitchen and open the biscuit tin. And there's the reward: the oh-so-delicious taste of your chocolate digestive. The whole thing is a never-ending loop: because of that tasty reward, you're more likely to experience the cue in future – and so the cycle continues.

But never fear: the bad-habit cycle isn't inevitable. Once you understand the science of habits, it becomes easier to build good behaviours and eradicate bad ones. The key is to hack into the habit loop – in particular, by fiddling with the 'cue' stage of the cycle.

To see this process in action, let's turn to the research of Peter Gollwitzer – a psychology professor at New York University whose work was popularised in *Switch*, an excellent book by the behavioural scientists Chip and Dan Heath.[9] Gollwitzer has long been intrigued by how we build consistent behaviour – and in particular, the often-jarring disconnect between what we say our goals are (stop eating biscuits) and what we actually do (eat more biscuits).

In his most famous study, Gollwitzer – along with a colleague, Veronika Brandstätter – set out to test when and how people are able to meet a goal. They told a group of students that they could earn extra marks in their studies if they wrote a paper about how they spent Christmas Eve. Easy, you might think. But, as with most such experiments, there was a catch: the paper had to be submitted by 26 December.

In the end, only a third of students actually submitted the paper. Fair enough: it was Christmas, after all. But Gollwitzer was more intrigued by which students *did* submit the test. You see, not all of the students had been given the same instructions. While some had just been sent a vague request – 'write a paper' – others had been invited to do something more specific. Upon being given the assignment, they were asked to note exactly where and when they would write it: 'I'll write this at the kitchen table on Christmas morning, before everyone else is awake,' for example.

The results were striking. Three-quarters of the students who had planned when and where they would write the report ended up submitting it – twice as many as the average.

Gollwitzer and Brandstätter have a less-than-catchy name for these prompts: 'implementation intentions'. They usually go by another name – action triggers. An action trigger is when you commit to do something at a set time. In practice, that means using the formula, '*When* I do X, *I will also* do Y.'

The genius of action triggers is that, used correctly, they can hack into the 'cue' stage of the habit loop. When Gollwitzer's students sat down at their breakfast table on Christmas morning, they suddenly remembered the paper they were supposed to be writing – the table itself became the cue. It's a powerful tool, and one that extends far beyond essay-writing. Consider the following examples:

When I have my breakfast, *I will* write my essay.
When I go to the shops, *I will* pop into the gym.

By settling on the right action triggers, you can build new behaviours into the fabric of your day. Even more powerfully, with a little tweaking these action triggers can be linked together – a process that the behaviour-change expert James Clear calls 'habit stacking'.[10] Try the formula '*After* I do X, *I will* do Y'.

After I get up, *I will* eat a piece of fruit for breakfast.
After I eat a piece of fruit for breakfast, *I will* brush my teeth.
After I brush my teeth, *I will* set off for the gym.

Using this method, a single, everyday cue – waking up in the morning – can be turned into a whole day's worth of positive actions. Habits take on their own momentum. One tiny decision creates a chain reaction of good behaviour.

Many of our high performers used action triggers in this manner. They built positive behavioural prompts into their day. And by identifying the right trigger points, they created a culture in which trademark behaviours come naturally.

A useful example comes from Tracey Neville's work with the England Roses. When she became manager, Neville issued an edict: the dressing room mattered. In many sports teams, the dressing room is considered the players' private domain and so, naturally, it can start to look like ground zero in a laundry explosion. But Neville thought that players' behaviour as they got dressed was a classic action trigger. If they were undisciplined in the changing room, they would be undisciplined on the pitch.

She took inspiration from the UCLA basketball coach John Wooden, who had strong views on how his players got dressed, down to how they put on their socks. 'Now run your hand around the little toe area ... make sure there are no wrinkles and then pull it back up,' Wooden would say. 'Check the heel area. We don't want any sign of a wrinkle about it ... The wrinkle will be sure you get blisters, and those blisters are going to make you lose playing time.'[11] Wooden's point was that getting dressed well would start a chain reaction that would lead to discipline on the court. The socks were an action trigger. And so too were Neville's lockers. She changed one cue in her players' day: before you leave the dressing room, tidy up your locker. This led to dozens of other positive behavioural cues through the day. The habit cycle continued.

Or take Shaun Wane. He told us how he would hold regular 7:00am meetings – giving particular kudos to players who turned up early. In the process, he kick-started a chain reaction. His players would learn that that going to bed early was the best way to get the boss's attention. This in turn led to greater discipline: they took a more regimented approach to their evening, and they found themselves thinking more about the next day, preparing themselves to give their all to the club. The habit cycle continued.

We can use this method in our own lives. Say your trademark behaviour is to never check Instagram when at work. Try to identify a trigger point early in your morning that will minimise the likelihood of any distractions. *After* I arrive at my desk, *I will* log out of all social media. *After* I log out of social media, *I will* turn my phone on to silent. These small behavioural cues help us commit to trademark behaviours in the long term.

HIGH PERFORMANCE PIT STOP – SHADOWS AND LIGHT

Damian

When you commit to a trademark behaviour, commit to it 100 per cent. Yes, practise the behaviour in those high-profile, high-pressure moments: when you're in an important meeting, or trying to win a match. But also practise the trademark behaviour when you're alone, when the pressure's off and nobody's watching.

Why? Well, as I sometimes put it to the athletes I coach: *what is done in the shadows reveals itself in the light*. If you have rehearsed your trademark behaviour in every waking moment – at work and at home, with colleagues and with family – you'll have learned to do it unthinkingly. Even when you're pushing yourself to the limit. Even when you're under unimaginable pressure.

What happens if we treat our trademark behaviours as a part-time hobby? Well, one boxer I trained found out the hard way. He was young, cocky and supremely talented. He had lightning reflexes, elastic-like movement and a rapier jab. His great flaw? He lacked commitment. Instead of getting up every morning to run, he would lie in. Instead of making sure he was on time to training, he'd rock up half an hour late. He knew what his trademark behaviours should be, but he didn't care.

Because of his natural talent, generally it didn't matter. Once he was in the boxing gym, he would take his trademark behaviours seriously. He'd still beat his sparring partners. He'd still outpace everybody he trained with.

Until, suddenly, it did matter. Our young boxer's innate skill took him as far as competing for a major title, where he was up against a much more experienced – but perhaps less talented – opponent. In the first six rounds of the fight, our boxer's superior abilities allowed him to establish a dominant lead.

But his opponent was committed, and he knew that the final six rounds would need a different skillset. As the two men got more tired, talent became less important – what mattered instead were grit, resolve and commitment. The victor would be the man who managed to press on through the pain.

After the fight, our boxer explained to me what had been going on in his head. He began searching his memory for evidence of his commitment – moments when he'd been more resilient than the rest, proven able to endure hardship. He searched in vain. And so he panicked. He lost the will to win, and found himself struggling to merely survive. The fight was lost.

> It was a succinct demonstration of the need for consistency. Your trademark behaviours can't be a part-time job. You need to commit to them every minute, every hour, every day. *What is done in the shadows reveals itself in the light.*

YOUR HIGH PERFORMANCE IDENTITY

It was 2000, and Rio Ferdinand's career had stalled. Everyone agreed he had the potential to become one of the country's greatest centre-backs – and everyone could see that he wasn't living up to it.

The issue was that he just couldn't focus. 'I found the bright lights of London and the invitations to nightclubs so hard to refuse,' Ferdinand said of his era playing for West Ham on the *High Performance* podcast. This period coincided with a drift in his form, which ended in a crushing disappointment – being left out of the England squad for the European Championships in 2000.

This shock was the beginning of a stunning turnaround. 'It was a wake-up call,' Ferdinand told us. And so he made a radical decision: to move from West Ham to Leeds United. Ferdinand wanted the move to be the start of something: his transformation from a high-potential player to a high-performing one. He asked Leeds manager, David O'Leary, what he was doing wrong – and what he should do instead: 'I asked him, "How can you help me improve as an elite footballer?"'

O'Leary came back with a long list. He prescribed nothing short of a rewiring of how Ferdinand thought about the game, himself and his opponents. For one thing, the distractions needed to stop – no more clubbing. For another, he needed to change his approach to football. 'I had to go into games with my mind right, ready and focused,' Ferdinand told us. 'I had to respect my opponents. I couldn't expect to switch my focus on and off like a lightbulb.'

 'I had to go into games with my mind right. I couldn't expect to switch my focus on and off like a lightbulb.' Rio Ferdinand

Above all, Ferdinand needed to start taking football seriously: 'I suddenly got it: this is a serious business and I need to make sure everything is on point.' The rest is history. Ferdinand's form transformed. In 2001, he became the Leeds captain; in 2002, he moved to Manchester United for a record-breaking £30 million transfer fee. He wouldn't miss the call-up from England for another ten years.

Ferdinand's story is a neat summary of the third step to building consistent, high performance behaviours. So far, we've explored how to identify your trademark behaviours and some neat methods for turning them into habits. But these methods are only a short-term solution. If we're serious about building consistent behaviours in the long term, we need nothing less than to change our sense of who we are.

You see, Ferdinand's problem wasn't that he wasn't sure of his trademark behaviours. It wasn't even that he was surrounded by the wrong cues (although those nightclubs probably didn't help). It was that he didn't think of himself as an elite player. Without the identity of a world-beating athlete, it was almost impossible to become one.

Psychologists have long argued that the route to sustained high performance is a shift in your identity. In the words of the bestselling book *Atomic Habits* by James Clear, 'Identity change is the North Star of habit change.'[12] If you don't think of yourself as a high performer, you'll never behave like one.

Say you saw a biscuit in the cupboard, and felt an urge to eat it. As you grapple with your instincts, your subconscious mind is reflecting on a hard question: 'What sort of person am I?' Are you the sort of person who would eat a biscuit? Are you someone who's good at resisting their urges? Are you someone who's committed to their health? In Ferdinand's case, the question was the same, even though the answer was different. 'What sort of person am I?' his subconscious asked him. The answer needed to be, 'The type of person who puts his sport above everything else.'

To understand why identity is so important, let's examine the work of James March, a professor of political science at Stanford University.[13] From early on in his career, March was intrigued by people who vote against their own self-interest: millionaires who voted for higher taxes, or people on benefits who voted for welfare cuts. Voters, he concluded, aren't nearly as 'rational' as we might think.

This led March to develop a new theory for how people actually make decisions, also described in Chip and Dan Heath's *Switch*.[14] We usually assume, March argues, that people are making decisions on the basis of the outcome. He calls this the 'consequences model'. It implies that when we have a decision to make, we mentally calculate the costs and the benefits of all of our options, then make the choice that increases our overall satisfaction. It assumes a cold, reasoned, analytical approach to choice.

But March said that this mode of reasoning isn't nearly as prevalent as you might think. In fact, he said, we usually make choices using the 'identity model'. In this mode, we're making calls by essentially asking ourselves three questions: who am I? What kind of situation is this? What would someone like me do in this situation? Identity is key: your sense of who you *are* determines what you *do*. When we're in this mode, we might not act strictly rationally. If you're a millionaire but you think of yourself as a compassionate, generous person, you could easily vote for a tax rise.

March argued that identity is the more powerful force in determining our decisions in the long term. If we think of ourselves as a certain type of person, we make decisions that chime with that identity. This is an essential lesson on our journey to high performance. If you want to build trademark behaviours in the long term, you need to change who you are.

We can see this process in action by looking at the career of Kelly Jones. When we sat down to talk with Jones, the singer-songwriter and gravel-voiced frontman of rock band Stereophonics, he explained how he had carved out an identity as a musician. The strength of this identity is what allowed him to commit to his trademark behaviours through thick and thin.

Like many creative people, Jones began to think of himself as an artist from a young age. Even as a child, he wasn't just someone who played music – he *was* a musician. 'My earliest memories are of making up little melodies that I knew weren't anybody else's,' he told us. 'I was probably about eight or nine years old.' As his childhood went on, this sense of himself as an artist only grew:

When I got to about twelve, I had a guitar and I started in a band, playing at a working men's club at the end of the street. We'd do Van Halen covers or Eagles covers, and sometimes we'd slot one of our own songs in between two very popular covers, to see if we could get away with it.

In the course of our interview, it became clear that Jones' identity as a musician had helped him during the toughest moments in his working life. His career had reached astonishing heights: 10 million sales, seven UK number one albums, twenty-three platinum sales awards, five BRIT nominations and one BRIT win. But it hadn't always been straightforward. Over the years, Jones had clashed with his crew, transformed his musical direction multiple times, even been told that Stereophonics would never again have a hit album. At every stage, his confidence in who he was – his identity as a musician – helped him persevere.

He told us, for example, of receiving a call from Bob Geldof in 2005. The rock star wanted Stereophonics to perform at Live 8 – the world's biggest concert in decades, created to call for action on global poverty. 'I jumped at it,' Jones told us. 'I was so excited.' But there was a hitch. Jones' crew didn't want to do it. Geldof had told Jones about some tricky logistical requirements – including the need to set up their equipment in just seven minutes. '"We can't do that," my crew told me,' he said. '"That's not possible for us. We can't do the show."'

What did Jones do? Well, he fell back on his identity as a musician. *Who am I? What kind of situation is this? What would someone like me do in this situation?* Jones knew that a world-class artist wouldn't let logistics stand in their way – and so he decided that he wouldn't either. 'I *could* do it,' he told us. 'I had spent years dedicated to learning my craft and I wasn't going to miss this once-in-a-lifetime opportunity simply because of my crew.' And so the show happened, just without the full set-up that

Stereophonics usually used. Jones knew that, if he was serious about being a generation-defining musician, he needed to press ahead in spite of what his crew said. 'I knew I was going to have to move on to the next level without them,' he told us.

Or take the time that Jones discovered he had a growth on his vocal cords. He had gone to the doctor for a regular check-up, only to discover he had a 'one-off trauma polyp' – the result of a bad cough or shouting in a football crowd, perhaps. They had to operate. 'I went in and they took it off, and then I had to go to Wales for a recovery,' Jones told us. The recovery was arduous: 'I couldn't speak for about three days, and then I could speak for two minutes, and then I could speak for five minutes ... It was quite a strange process.' Worst of all, he found himself unable to sing.

How did Jones get through it? He drew on his identity. *Who am I? What kind of situation is this? What would someone like me do in this situation?* If Jones was a true musician, he would do anything to get back the skill that had made him who he was. And so he did. 'I had to go through all this very slow process, and try to regain the strength,' Jones told us. 'The surgeon put me in touch with Joshua [a vocal coach], and then I set about learning literally how to sing again.' And sure enough, with time, his voice recovered.

Jones is a striking example of the power of identity. Once we see a behaviour as part of who we are, it allows us to persevere with it in spite of everything – whatever life throws at us. Jones' trademark behaviours – singing every day, writing every week – were completely integrated into his sense of self, and so he didn't need to think about whether to enact them, or require any external validation to commit to them. 'I genuinely don't care if anybody is interested in it, or likes it,' Jones said of his music. 'I just want to get it out.' Music is who he is.

We can all learn from Jones' example. If you're serious about building a behaviour in the long term, try not to frame it as a one-off choice. Frame it as a series of questions about the type of person you want to be. *Who am I? What kind of situation is this? What would someone like me do in this situation?*

NEVER MISS TWICE

'From the minute that they get up to the breakfast that they take. The water they take in their car on the way to training, to get their hydration right ... They go into a training ground, never late. They wear the right clothes. It's that consistency.'

Phil Neville was offering one of the most impassioned descriptions of high performance that we had heard. His worldview emphasised one principle above all else: consistency. Or, as Neville put it, 'Doing the right thing – every single minute of every single day.'

Of our high performers, Neville's emphasis on consistency was the most explicit. But he was far from the only person to mention it. As we've seen in this chapter, high performers ranging from cyclists to netball coaches, rugby league managers to rock stars, know the power of commitment. They told us about the need to identify your trademark behaviours. They talked us through how they committed to them. And they described rehearsing them again and again – from morning to night, at home and at work.

Yet one question remains. You might be thinking: what happens if I *do* slip up? Many of our high performers were mindful of this issue too. Sure, they emphasised the need for consistency. But they acknowledged that nobody could be consistent all the time. We're all human. Even Phil Neville.

In the closing section of our podcast, we've taken to asking our interviewees a simple question: how did you react to your greatest failure? The answers are invariably fascinating. Ben Ainslie told us he reviewed the failure in his head and tried not to repeat it. Ole Gunnar Solskjær said failure had always spurred him to do something about it. Frank Lampard had the most amusing answer: 'Which one of my failures do you want to choose?'

The truth is, everybody fails sometimes – even the world's greatest athletes and entrepreneurs. You might turn up late one day in a hundred. You might miss a training session that you said you'd attend. It happens.

High performance isn't about never failing. It's about how you respond to that first failure.

James Clear, the habits expert we referred to earlier, has a simple maxim for responding to these inevitable, occasional slip-ups: 'Never miss twice.'[15] He argues that missing a habit once isn't the end of the world and doesn't affect what you do in the long term. The trick is to immediately get back on track.

And so high performers aim for these slip-ups to be a comma, rather than a full stop. Errors offer us the chance to pause, reflect and try again. It's not failing once that gets you – it's failing twice, three times or even four. As Clear puts it, 'One mistake is just an outlier. Two mistakes is the beginning of a pattern.' This is our final lesson on consistency. If you spot yourself erring from your trademark behaviour try not to panic – just don't err a second time.

In the course of your high performance journey, your commitment to your trademark behaviours will be tested to its limits. Sometimes, you might not live up to them. It's not the end of the world. But if you do slip up, it's your responsibility to come back swinging. Never be late a second time. Never skip your second training session. Never miss twice.

LESSON SUMMARY

- High performers are consistent. They have a handful of non-negotiable trademark behaviours – and they stick to them.
- To find your trademarks, remember Shaun Wane's formula: they should be simple, they should count under pressure, and they should be clear.
- To make your trademarks effective, turn them into habits – by building behavioural cues (or 'action triggers') into your environment.
- To make your trademarks long-lasting, build them into your identity. Imagine an ideal version of yourself and ask: *What would they do in this situation?*
- Above all, remember this simple motto: Never miss twice. Yes, on some days your habits might slip. But if high performers miss one day, they never miss a second.

High Performance Teams

None of us succeeds or fails by ourselves. We succeed or fail as a group. And groups need to be led.

LEAD THE TEAM

'Since I have been alive, I have never seen South Africa like this.'

It was the 2019 Rugby World Cup in Japan, and Siya Kolisi – captain of the victorious Springboks – was speaking from the pitch moments after beating England in the final. Over the previous eighty minutes, his squad had methodically dismantled England's hopes of winning the tournament. Now, International Stadium Yokohama had fallen silent, its crowds gripped by the words of South Africa's talismanic leader: 'We really appreciate all the support: people in the taverns, people in the shebeens, people on farms, homeless people ... We love you South Africa and we can achieve anything if we work together as one.'[1]

Over the previous eighteen months, Kolisi had led the South Africa rugby team through one of the most extraordinary periods in its history. When Rassie Erasmus was appointed head coach in March 2018, the team had been in disarray, having won just eleven of their previous twenty-five test matches. Just a year later, and their captain was lifting the Webb Ellis Cup.

Yet even more remarkable was what Kolisi's captaincy represented. Rugby had long embodied the toxic legacy of apartheid. Until the end of segregation in the mid-1990s, the Springboks had been an entirely white team. Even in the years after apartheid, rugby had remained a largely white sport – even after the country's first Black president, Nelson Mandela, presented the trophy to the home team at the 1995 World Cup in South Africa. For all the talk of a post-apartheid 'rainbow nation', the 1995 champions had only one Black player in their starting fifteen – hardly representative of a country that was 80 per cent Black and only 10 per cent white. A few years later, three months before the start of the 1999 World Cup, South Africa played Wales with an all-white starting XV.

Change would come, but it would take time. In 1999, South Africa's president Thabo Mbeki declared the 1999 Springboks would be the last all-white team. By 2007, the team that won the World Cup had two players of colour. In 2017, Erasmus – then the club's director of rugby – announced his intention to put things right. Six months after his appointment, he made Kolisi captain – the first Black leader of the team in its 130-year history.

When we sat down with Kolisi on the *High Performance* podcast, it was clear that he embodied everything that a leader should be: charismatic, single-minded, and with a unique knack for bringing people together – particularly important for a team with as troubled a history as the Springboks.

But his journey to leadership had been an unlikely one. Growing up in 1990s Zwide, a township in Port Elizabeth, the notion that Kolisi would one day lead his national team to victory would have seemed fanciful. He lived in a house with his grandmother, uncle, aunt, and their two children. 'When I was in the township, when my grandma was still alive, I didn't imagine or think I was going to make it out of that,' he told us.

His childhood wasn't unhappy: 'I was living in the moment,' he told us. 'I struggled financially, I couldn't get food and all that stuff. But I was rich. I had love for my grandmother … And that is all I needed at that time.' It was never easy, though. 'When I got a meal, I got a meal, you know? I just focused on what I had, used as much as I could,' he recalled.

From an early age, it was clear Kolisi had a remarkable talent. At the age of ten, he was playing in a kids' rugby game. Eric Songwiqi, principal of the nearby Emsengeni Primary School, was watching. He invited Kolisi to move to his school, where he was a part-time rugby coach. Shortly afterwards, Kolisi was offered a full rugby scholarship to Grey High School – one of the most prestigious boarding schools in South Africa.

This new environment was challenging. Kolisi spoke Xhosa; the classes were taught in English. And the privileged students around Kolisi had had very different lives from his. But he was determined to make the most of being at Grey. He told us about his mentality in those formative years: 'You've got to work. You've got to work each and every single day.'

That meant he was prepared to take advantage of everything the school had to offer. 'When the opportunity came, I was ready,' he told us. 'Most people complain and complain and complain. Opportunity presents itself, and they're not ready. And that's what the difference is: every single time I've had an opportunity, I've been able to grab it with both hands.' And ready Kolisi was – when he was offered his scholarship, when he began his youth career playing for Eastern Province Kings in 2007 and, of course, when he received the call-up for the South African national team in 2013.

'Most people complain and complain and complain. Opportunity presents itself, and they're not ready.' Siya Kolisi

We could see that Kolisi had a knack for inspiring people. His goal was not to represent any one race or class of South African – but to represent everyone. 'I'm not only trying to inspire Black kids but people from all races,' he once said. 'When I'm on the field and I look into the crowd, I see people of all races and social classes. We as players represent the whole country.'[2]

He was no ordinary leader. With time, Kolisi would become known for his reserved, quietly confident style of leadership. We asked him about it on the podcast, and he said it came naturally. 'That's just who I am ... I'm quiet because we have different leaders in our group,' he said. 'Because I'm so sure in myself, I know who I am and what I stand for, and what type of leader I am.' This style of quiet leadership would forge a team like no other – a group who would remain united in the face of extraordinary adversity.

The documentary *Chasing the Sun*, which depicts Springboks' world cup successes in Japan, offers a glimpse of this atmosphere. In one scene, Erasmus has asked every player to supply photos of their friends and family. But one member of the squad, Makazole Mapimpi, had brought only photos of himself. His teammates seem perplexed – until Mapimpi explains. His 'real' family are dead: his mother killed in a car-crash, his brother lost to a brain illness. The only family he has are Springboks, he says.

Many commentators have said that such close emotional bonds within the team helps explains their success. And many of these bonds were down to Kolisi.

In the build up to that fateful final in Yokohoma in November, 2019, Erasmus emphasised the importance of Kolisi's leadership. He said his players were uniquely well placed to deal with pressure – after all, many of them came from a world in which having to go without food, or having to walk six miles to school every day, was routine. Why would they be worried about the

World Cup final? According to Erasmus, Kolisi embodied this resilience better than anyone. 'This man has known those pressures,' he said.[3]

The next evening in Yokohama, as South Africa demolished England's hopes of regaining the trophy, the Springboks were unrecognisable from the almost entirely white team of fifteen years earlier. There were eleven Black players in Kolisi's squad. Mapimpi made history as South Africa's first ever try scorer in a World Cup final, the scoring pass to him provided by another township boy, Lukhanyo Am. The revolution in South African rugby was complete.

Kolisi's story is a succinct demonstration of the power of inspirational leadership. It is one of the final pieces in the puzzle of high performance. So far in this book, we've discussed how to become a high-achieving individual – from examining the idiosyncratic ways high performers think, to exploring the peculiar ways they act. But there's something missing. None of us succeeds or fails by ourselves. We succeed or fail as a group. And groups need to be led.

The power of effective teams is difficult to overstate. The evidence is overwhelming. In one seminal study from 1920, Floyd Henry Allport – often described as the founder of social psychology – set out to investigate how being part of a group affects people's intelligence. And so he asked a group of people to undertake a set of simple puzzles twice in a row. The first time, they were working alone; the second time they were also working individually, but were sat on a table with a group of others.

What he found was astonishing. Working around other people was by itself enough to boost performance.[4] It didn't matter whether the participants were communicating or sitting in silence, close friends or complete strangers – the very fact of being part of a team made people smarter.

Even more intriguingly, well-run teams of low perform-ers consistently do better work than badly run teams of high performers. In one entertainingly wide-ranging study, academ-ics at Northwestern University set out to investigate the notion that the more talent you have, the better a team will do. They investigated the role of talent in a variety of leagues: the NBA, the Premier League, Major League Baseball and, naturally, the multiplayer online battle game *Defense of the Ancients 2*. Their findings were counter-intuitive. Yes, the talent of individuals in a team counted for something, but the best predictor of a team's outcome was *shared* success between team members – that is, it was down to good teamwork.[5]

As the co-founder of LinkedIn, Reid Hoffman, put it, 'No matter how brilliant your mind or strategy, if you're playing a solo game, you'll always lose out to a team.'[6]

All this means that if you're serious about high performance, you need to get serious about boosting your team. And that's what the final section of this book is about. We'll explore why some groups come together to produce brilliant work – and why others don't.

This is where the story of Siya Kolisi comes in. His inspiring captaincy of the Springboks hints at the first key way to make a team excel – effective leadership. When a group has good leadership – as in the case of Kolisi's Springboks – something extraordinary happens. Middling members of the team become high performers; good members of the team players become superstars.

But Kolisi's captaincy also hints at how we get leadership wrong. Far from being a domineering, controlling leader, Kolisi merely set his club's direction – knowing that, with the right prompts, his squad would achieve high performance on their own terms. And far from being a solitary figure, alone at the top,

Kolisi decided to draw on his teammates' skill wherever possible, with lieutenants such as Mapimpi and Am. The result is a different picture of leadership to the one you might imagine. Good leaders rarely command and control. Instead, they set a group's direction – and trust their team to deliver the goods.

FIND YOUR BHAG

In their seminal study of long-lasting organisations, *Built to Last*, the management academics Jim Collins and Jerry Porras coined a memorable term: BHAG. It stands for 'Big, Hairy, Audacious Goal'.

Collins and Porras defined a BHAG as 'an audacious ten-to-thirty-year goal to progress towards an envisioned future'. Their research showed that massive, motivating objectives distinguish good companies from brilliant ones. The best goals should be immediately attention-grabbing – they 'hit you in the gut', the pair said.[7]

Since Collins and Porras coined the term, dozens of researchers have investigated their power – including the American psychologists Chip and Dan Heath.[8] They say BHAGs' power lies in convincing everyone to focus on a goal that is so massive that it can't help but inspire.

Henry Ford's BHAG from the 1910s and 1920s was to 'democratise the automobile'. Tick.

Walmart's BHAG, agreed in 1990, was to quadruple in size to be a $125 billion company by the year 2000. Tick.

Boeing's BHAG, settled on in 1952, was to become the market leader in creating commercial jets. Tick.

There's a lesson here about the power of leadership. The first role of a leader is to set a direction for your team – by identifying what you are trying to achieve. And you need to be bold. If you don't have a BHAG, you're unlikely to be able to unite the team in pursuit of a shared objective.

In the course of our *High Performance* interviews, the power of 'BHAG leadership' has come up time and time again. Sean Dyche offers perhaps the best example. When he became manager of Burnley in 2012, Dyche felt the club was missing a sense of direction. The team had been languishing in the Championship, and had been through a tough few years – experiencing the short-lived jubilation of promotion into the Premier League, before quickly being relegated back down again.

The late 2000s, Dyche thought, had been a wasted opportunity. In his first board meeting as head coach, Dyche asked the board where all the money had gone after the club's sole season in the Premier League in 2009–10. The stadium was run down, the dressing rooms untouched since his time as a player twenty years previously. 'The training pitches were still average at best and I was like, "Where has the money gone?"' he said in one interview.[9]

In Dyche's view, the issue was a lack of focus: the club had no clear objective. He told us about visiting the Oxford University rowing team when he was training to be a coach. They were getting ready for the annual Boat Race against Cambridge. 'They were non-professionals who were the most professional people I've ever seen,' he told us of the students on the team. 'They just had a blackboard with literally the date and the time of the Boat Race written on it. Not some trendy amazing poster with lights around it – just a blackboard.' Dyche realised every team should aim for this kind of clarity. What was the team's objective? To win the Boat Race. So what did they do? They focused on winning the Boat Race.

In time, a similar approach would inform Dyche's strategy at Burnley. They needed clarity, he thought, and the best way to get it was through a good old-fashioned BHAG. Dyche concluded that the most important, audacious thing that Burnley could aim for was to fight its way back into the Premier League – and this time not just to go up, but stay up. When he proposed this particular goal, it seemed optimistic. Burnley had nearly plummeted out of the entire football league just a couple of decades earlier, and had just been relegated from the Premier League. But Dyche realised that without lofty ambitions, Burnley's trajectory would only be downwards.

This ambition proved to be just what the club needed. It focused the minds of the management, the team and even the fans – just like that blackboard Dyche had seen in Oxford. The goal wasn't just for the next year, or even five years – it was for the next few decades. 'Everyone bought into the idea of it being a chance to structure the club not for year one but for twenty-five years,' Dyche would say later.[10]

This kind of long-term thinking informed how Dyche approached the club's stadium, Turf Moor. Dyche believed that if Burnley were to think like a Premier League club, they needed to look like one too. And so he convinced the management to invest in the club's grounds – not just revitalising the pitch, but also creating new floodlights, erecting disability stands, improving internet connectivity for broadcasters and even creating new seats in the away end. This commitment to investing in the club for the long term – and hence putting money into its physical infrastructure, rather than just its players – was a crucial part of his BHAG.

At the same time, Dyche developed a long-term strategy for the squad. His approach to buying players wasn't about the coming season. It was about the coming decades – building up players, buying them relatively cheaply and keeping them with the team. 'This is not a club that wants to sign foreign players for

£20 million and then sell them two years later for £7 million,' he told us. 'This club is built on trying to buy players who we know stuff about, and we can develop them. Maybe they grow older being part of the club.'

However, the cleverest thing about Dyche was how he converted his BHAG into more manageable, short-term behaviours. The trick here was avoiding micro-management. His strategy was simple: Rather than obsessively telling every player what to do at every moment, identify a handful of all-important behaviours – trademark behaviours – and emphasise them above all else.

In many areas, Dyche was a chilled-out manager. 'The negotiables are wide and varied – the lads know that, they can't name them all,' he told us of the team's behaviours. But there were a few critical areas where there was zero ambiguity: 'There's way less non-negotiables – certain things are important.' Provided they agreed to a handful of trademark behaviours, Dyche trusted his team to get the job done on their own terms.

 'The negotiables are wide and varied. There's way less non-negotiables – certain things are important.' Sean Dyche

During our conversation, we spotted three non-negotiable behaviours pinned on the walls:

'Noses point in the same direction'

'The minimum requirement is maximum effort'

'Give us your legs, hearts and minds'

There's a remarkable elegance to Dyche's trademark behaviours. Each of the concepts is discrete and clear. And they are all-encompassing – it's hard to think of a situation in which these behaviours can't offer guidance.

Everything Dyche did was about emphasising these trademarks. He started organising his training so that they were an inescapable feature of his teams' lives. Most famously, he created a unique test which all of his players have to successfully navigate. It is known within the club as 'Gaffer's Day' – a day when the three non-negotiable behaviours come above everything else.

The reputation of Gaffer's Day was fearsome. Jason Shackell, the former Burnley club captain, once described how Dyche would warn his players to be prepared: 'Get ready for my day,' he would say throughout the year. For many, it was a mysterious – even ominous – occasion. 'I'd heard about this Gaffer's Day,' the player David Jones once said. Jones arrived to a pitch that was empty, apart from a few tractor tyres. 'I hadn't worked with him before,' Jones explained, 'and your mind starts going into overdrive thinking, "what's going to happen here today?"'[11]

The answer was simple – on Gaffer's Day, everyone's endurance would be tested to the limits. 'It was a day without science,' recounted Shackell. 'We ran until we were dead, basically, and then called it a day.'[12] That meant hours upon hours of pure fitness work and intense running, not a football in sight. It was exhausting: 'It is about taking them right to the edges of their physical capability,' Dyche explained to us.

Why did Dyche force his team to go through such an ordeal? The answer, of course, relates back to his BHAG. 'You cannot complete it successfully without commitment, teamwork and sheer hard work,' he laughed. And once this mentality was inculcated in training, it would stick in the minds of players through their matches.

Overall, Dyche's method is compellingly straightforward. Identify your team's goal, identify a small number of behaviours that will help them achieve it, then trust your team to do the rest. It's the opposite of micro-management – macro-management perhaps. The leader's job isn't to control every facet of a team's behaviour. It is to identify a BHAG, and pinpoint the handful of behaviours that will get the team there. And it works. At the time of writing, Burnley has been in the Premier League for five consecutive years.

HIGH PERFORMANCE PIT STOP – COMMANDER'S INTENT

The Commander's Intent is a clear, straightforward statement that is included in every written order given in the US Army.[13] It specifies the goal of an operation. And though it rarely specifies the precise actions a team should take, it describes the behaviours that soldiers might be required to exhibit. It's the same principle as Sean Dyche's: set a finite number of unambiguous behaviours, and let your squad handle the rest.

In particular, the Commander's Intent includes two instructions for officers. Broadly, they conform to the following pattern – officers must fill in the blanks:

The objective of tomorrow's mission is to:

_____

The single most important thing we can do to achieve it is:

_____

It's a quickfire way to identify your objective and work out how to achieve it, US Army – or Burnley FC – style. First comes the goal, next comes the behaviour.

Try applying this method to a problem you're facing in your own life. What is the objective of your mission? And what can you do to reach it?

CUT OUT THE BULLSHIT

BHAGs are only the first ingredient in the recipe for effective leadership. Being a leader isn't just about encouraging good behaviours. It's also about discouraging bad ones.

To understand why, let's return to the work of Jim Collins. When he was a graduate student, a professor taught Collins a harsh but valuable lesson. He was always busy, she said, but that didn't mean he was doing anything right. She asked him how he would change his behaviour if he received two life-changing phone calls. In the first, he'd learn that he had inherited $20 million, no strings attached. In the second, he'd learn that, due to a rare and incurable disease, he had only ten years left to live. In that situation, she asked him, 'What would you stop doing?' (In Collins' case, the answer was: quite a lot.)

This thought experiment gets you to focus on what really matters. Just such an emphasis on the essential – and eradication of the inessential – is one of the key characteristics of the best teams, Collins says. 'A great piece of art is composed not just of what is in the final piece, but equally important, what is not,' he writes. 'It is the discipline to discard what does not fit ... [that] marks the ideal piece of work, be it a symphony, a novel, a painting, a company or, most important of all, a life.'[14]

And so our second principle of good leadership is the flipside of the first: cut out the bullshit. This is a lesson that many of our high performers have mentioned on the podcast. 'Saying "no" is a critical skill,' Tom Daley told us. 'It allows complete focus on the most important stuff.' It's an outlook that many of the world's most remarkable individuals share. There's a story – perhaps apocryphal – of the Beatles' drummer Ringo Starr describing the art of great drumming as 'knowing when *not* to hit the drum'.

'Saying "no" is a critical skill. It allows complete focus on the most important stuff.' Tom Daley

Yet even the best sportspeople, businesspeople and creatives neglect this lesson. Most of us get distracted by unimportant tasks all the time. In one amusing study conducted by the leadership expert Peter Bregman, a group of managers were asked to share the important problems they were facing in their organisations. Most managers mentioned five to eight issues. Next, they were asked to describe their activities from the previous week. The kicker came in the conclusion: 'No manager reported any activity which could be directly associated with the problems they had described,' it said.[15] The issue is one that most of us are familiar with: urgent tasks get prioritised over important ones.

So, what can leaders do to eradicate the pointless tasks that erode a team's performance? This was a question that Ben Francis found himself asking regularly. In the end, it led him to radically re-evaluate his role in the company he founded.

Francis' career is one of the great success stories of recent business. He was ambitious from early on. At the age of fourteen, he completed some work experience with his grandfather, whose company lined industrial furnaces. The gruelling job didn't tickle his fancy as a career, but it did teach him the value of hard work. 'The first job I had was working with him, so I definitely got a work ethic from those guys,' he told us.

A self-proclaimed 'very average' student, during his teenage years Francis discovered his real passions – IT on the one hand, the gym on the other. He became obsessed with YouTube weight-lifting clips of icons like Arnold Schwarzenegger. By the age of eighteen, he had noticed a gap in the market: the more he worked out, the harder he found it to find a shirt that would properly show off his muscles. By the time he had begun his undergraduate degree in Birmingham, he had started ripping t-shirts into Schwarzenegger-style tank tops – and decking them out with his logo, a great white shark lifting a barbell.

Therein lay a billion-pound business idea. In 2012, at the age of nineteen, Francis founded Gymshark – a company that sold branded shirts and protein shakes. In the early days it was low-tech: a friend taught him to screen-print t-shirts, and his grandmother taught him how to sew. 'Nothing was particularly strategic,' he said later. 'It was just me and some friends thinking that no one else was making what we wanted to wear.'[16]

But, as the company grew, Francis would become more business savvy. The clothes were taking off – particularly among online fitness influencers. Followers were soon asking where they'd bought them. This was 2013, when 'influencer marketing' on social media was still in its earliest days. But it is exactly what Francis was pioneering. Over the next few years, his company would grow exponentially, largely thanks to the support of these online advocates. By 2021, the company was selling 20 million items a year – an average of more than 50,000 per day – and had a value of over £1 billion.

Yet for much of this period, Francis was not the CEO of the company he had founded. And it was all thanks to an epiphany that Jim Collins would approve of – the need to stop doing things that aren't right for your team. In 2020, Francis posted a blog explaining his journey. 'When you're the founder and majority shareholder of a business, you end up becoming a weird amalgamation of a number of different roles,' he wrote. 'You end up becoming a bit of a player manager. Someone who acts and works in the business, but someone who's also a part of deciding who works (or plays), where.'[17]

On the podcast, Francis described gradually realising that there were elements of the CEO job he needed to eliminate. The discovery came following the recruitment of two new senior colleagues. Steve Hewitt, a businessman almost twenty years Francis' senior, joined Gymshark as managing director and transformed the company's operations. 'Steve is utterly brilliant with people management, finance operations, logistics and things like that,' Francis told us. Meanwhile Paul Richardson came in as chairman. 'He was really thinking about the structure of business,' said Francis. It led to an epiphany: 'I could watch these two guys and realise: they were brilliant at the things I was terrible at.'

And so Francis did something radical. In 2017, after five years at the helm, Francis stood down as CEO in favour of Hewitt. The move allowed Francis to focus on the things he loved. 'I could double down and focus on brand, product, marketing, socials, all these sorts of things – and allow those guys to work on their strengths,' he said. And so Francis became chief marketing officer, as well as the public face of the company. His decision to focus on what he loves won him huge acclaim. Francis was named in *Forbes*' '30 Under 30', and he won the UK's best entrepreneur award in 2020.

What can we all learn from Francis' decision? First, good leadership is rarely about doing everything yourself. It's about trusting those around you – just like Sean Dyche had at Burnley. Leaders don't demand absolute control: they delegate. Sometimes, they give up their power and hand it to their teams. 'You need to set your ego aside and ensure the business is always put first, and the people strongest for each role are in those roles,' Francis once said.[18] If you applied this lesson to your team, what would you cut out?

 'You need to set your ego aside and ensure the business is always put first.' Ben Francis

Second, we should all focus on what we are actually good at – and eliminate everything else. This operates on an individual level – in Francis' case, his true calling was marketing. But it has ramifications for how an entire organisation is run. Is everybody focusing on what they do best, or are there parts of the team constantly getting derailed by non-essential tasks? Reflecting on this question can be liberating. Francis describes the decision to let Hewitt be CEO as 'extremely freeing'. 'It allowed me to focus on the things I excel at, [and] allowed Steve to focus on what he excels at – putting the business first, and allowing the business to grow even more quickly,' he wrote on his blog.[19]

Third, and most surprisingly, cutting things out in the short term is often the best way to keep your options open in the long term. When we spoke to Francis in summer 2021, he had just returned to his original role as CEO after four years away. But this time, he was ready. 'I'm the most excited I've ever been. I absolutely love it,' he told us. And that was all because he'd taken a step back four years previously – a process that allowed him to reflect, learn and progress. It was all down to knowing what, and when, to quit.

HIGH PERFORMANCE PIT STOP –
THE TO-DON'T LIST

This exercise offers a practical way to cut out tasks that don't matter. It takes its inspiration from what Jim Collins calls a 'stop-doing list'. Write down a list of everything you've done at work in the past week, focusing on tasks that take more than one hour. Next, go through that list and give it a mark out of ten for how much it aligns with your goals – or, even better, your BHAG.

These scores can form the basis of your 'stop-doing' list. You can then divide the tasks into three categories based on the score given to them.

For scores of 1–3: *stop it*. If a task isn't adding anything to your objectives, ask yourself whether you can stop doing it. Should you really be scrolling through your Instagram feed again?

For scores of 4–7: *delegate it*. If a task is inescapable but clearly isn't helping with your objectives, try to work out if there's a way to systematically remove it from your to-do list. Could you delegate it to another member of the team? Or, if you're working in a business, could you give the task to a freelancer?

For scores of 8–10: *focus on it*. If a task is in this top tier it should make up the bulk of your working hours. Is there a way to build these jobs into your rota – blocking out time every week to work on them, for example?

Of course, there will be exceptions – there are some tasks that are both enragingly pointless and unavoidable. But this is a useful starting point when it comes to turning your to-do list into a to-don't list.

FIND YOUR LIEUTENANTS

Something strange happens when you put people in groups. When we're by ourselves, we tend to act fairly rationally. But as soon as we're around others, we start to succumb to the pressure of the group. All that reasonableness goes out the window.

This is a phenomenon that the psychologist Solomon Asch was obsessed with. One of the pioneers of social psychology, Asch developed an interest in how we are swayed by the actions of our peers. In his most famous experiment, he asked a group of students to look at a number of simple drawings – including the below.

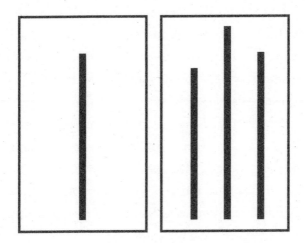

For each, they were asked a simple question. For example, when presented with the above illustration, they were asked which of the three lines on the right was most like the one on the left? The answer, in all cases, was clear. (It's the one on the far right. Obviously.)

Except there was a catch. All but one of the people in the room was a stooge – they had been paid to give the same, clearly wrong, answer. At the end of the experiment, the sole real subject was called upon to give their verdict. Terrifyingly, in three-quarters of cases, they went with the wrong answer at least once – just to fit in with the people around them.[20]

Asch's experiment would become one of the most famous experiments in history, a single-study proof of the power of peer pressure. It revealed how susceptible we all are to the behaviour of those around us – so much so that we're prepared to ignore the evidence before our eyes. Since Asch's day, similar experiments have been repeated in dozens of similar settings. All too frequently, people go with the crowd – even when that means ignoring the evidence before them.

Asch's findings on conformity are famous – many readers will be familiar with them already. But less famous are the exceptions to this rule. Because Solomon Asch didn't just identify when peer pressure did work; he also identified when it didn't.

In one of his less-well-known experiments, Asch briefed another room full of actors to give the wrong answers to a set of puzzles. But this time, there was a twist: he asked one of the actors to give a dissenting answer – the correct one. This lone voice of reason changed things. In many cases, it gave the non-actor in the room the 'permission' to break ranks, and offer the correct answer instead. 'The presence of a supporting power depleted the majority of much of its power,' Asch wrote. In fact, people became four times less likely to give the wrong answer when just one person gave the right one.[21]

Asch's experiments reveal the power of both peer pressure and of leadership. Regardless of how strong-willed we think we are, we are all tempted to follow the group. But you only need one leader to do things differently and the whole dynamic of a team can alter.

The Norwegian sports psychologist Willi Railo had a term for the individuals with this power: 'cultural architects'. They are the people who set an example for the rest of the group. 'Cultural architects are people who are able to change the mindset of others,' Railo said. 'They are able to break barriers, they have visions. They are self-confident and able to transfer self-confidence to other players.' In sport, cultural architects are the members of the team who set the tone in the dressing room; in business, they're the well-liked colleagues who new joiners look up to. Many of our high performers emphasised their importance. Ole Gunnar Solskjær put it most simply: a cultural architect is 'someone you look up to, someone with the right habits and standards.' You have to find these people and use them.[22]

'A cultural architect is someone you look up to.' Ole Gunnar Solskjær

How can leaders identify these cultural architects? This is a question we've asked many high performers – and the answers they've come back with have been remarkably consistent. Cultural architects are marked out by three characteristics: their status, their attitude and their talent.

First up, status. Instead of telling people what to do, these architects have an influence through their actions – people look up to them. They lead through status, rather than through instruction. For example, Phil Neville described joining Manchester United as a teenager and watching how Eric Cantona held himself. 'He did not speak so much, but led by example,' he told us. 'He was always very professional ... He trained hard and played hard and behaved correctly off the pitch too, in the spirit of the culture of the club.'

In time, Neville would come to have this effect on his own team. When he left Manchester United to join Everton, he explained how the habits he had adopted at his previous club – such as arriving early and warming up in the gym – were a culture shock to his new teammates. 'I was the only one doing it,' he said. But in this instance, he became a cultural architect himself – causing 'ripples' of behaviour change to pass through a team: 'Within my first two weeks at Everton, a small but committed group of senior players began to come in the gym with me and the ripples eventually meant everyone was doing it.' He knew that leading by example in this way could be transformative. 'When you have this group in a dressing room who understand what it means to be a part of a winning culture, this helps make an unstoppable force.'

Second is attitude. When we spoke to Chris Hoy, we suggested he may have been a cultural architect in Team GB. He was modest, at first brushing off the suggestion. But the more we talked, the more convinced we became. Why? Because of his attitude to his teammates. He had an unusually nurturing approach to more junior members of the group. 'I'm a lot older than them for a start,' he told us. 'I started out as the youngest member of the team, finished as the oldest.'

And that meant that he was happy to look after younger team-mates – like the British-German cyclist Phil Hindes: 'He came from Germany – he's got British parents, but he was born and raised in Germany. So he had to adapt to a whole new environment, a whole different country.' Hoy knew what to do. 'Basically I took him under my wing and tried to help him integrate into the team,' he told us. This, too, is another clue about who your cultural architects are – seek out those who protect, even nurture, other members of the team. Their attitude will build the environment you need to thrive.

Third, and most important, is talent. Cultural architects are the individuals who get their teammates' attention – and respect – through their sheer skill. Sean Dyche was particularly vocal on this point. He spoke of the difference between football leadership when he was a player in the 1990s and now. In those days, he said, leaders were more bolshie: 'They were pretty stand up, they'd have a laugh but know when to be serious.'

Today, however, leaders are more likely to inspire people through talent alone. 'Leadership's changed now,' Dyche said. 'The first kind of leadership shift I noticed was like David Beckham. You thought, *He's definitely not going to be leading through his words and all that stuff.* But he's going to be a leader through the fact that you put him on a football pitch and he's going to give you everything, and do it with a bit of style and a bit of class.' The cultural architects are those who impress through their skill first and foremost – and so set the tone for the group.

All this leads to our final principle of high performance leadership: find your lieutenants. The most successful leaders are those who draw upon a network of cultural architects – individuals who can take up the mantle of leadership, even when the leader isn't there.

These individuals reveal that leadership isn't as solitary as you might think. Because it's not a top-down process. Leadership is about fostering an environment in which people feel empowered – so that other leaders crop up all around you.

HIGH PERFORMANCE PIT STOP –
ARCHITECTS IN ACTION

Jake

It was a sunny spring afternoon in March 2014, and I was standing pitch-side at the Etihad Stadium, home to Manchester City. I'd been sent there to present City's match against Wigan Athletic in the FA Cup Quarter Final. According to the bookies, the hosts were odds-on to win.

Wigan Athletic had other ideas. Perhaps City were spooked by Wigan's record from the previous year – when the club had unexpectedly seen off City in the final to lift the FA Cup. Or maybe the hosts were just unlucky. Either way, Wigan won the match 2–1 – in large part thanks to a poor performance by veteran City defender Martín Demichelis.

Wigan's boss, Uwe Rösler, was in a good mood when he joined us for a chat after the game. But there was perhaps a tinge of regret – before becoming a coach, Rösler had played for Manchester City for half a decade, even naming his son after the Manchester City hero Colin Bell.

I thought this gave me the chance to be clever. 'You named one of your children Colin, after Colin Bell. Perhaps you'll name one Martín, after the City defender won you the game today,' I joked. It was childish and not very funny – though I didn't realise that at the time. Rösler handled my pettiness with characteristic grace, brushing off the question.

As we carried on with our post-match programme, however, I noticed something unusual. Lurking just a few yards behind the camera operators stood the Manchester City and England goalkeeper Joe Hart. 'He seems super pissed off with someone,' my co-presenter whispered. 'And I think he's looking at you.'

As we counted down to going off air, I began to feel anxious. I had a hunch what was going on. When I put down the mic, and started to walk off set, a press officer approached: 'Hi Jake, Joe would like a word if you don't mind?' Gulp. The three of us made our way into an office in the bowels of the stadium.

I'm a tall bloke, six foot four, almost sixteen stone, yet I felt about two foot nothing standing in front of Joe Hart. 'What are you trying to do?' he asked. He was referring to my jibe at Demichelis. 'How do you think he feels seeing that after the day he has had?' I offered a meek counter-argument about my job being to offer entertainment, but I knew Hart was right.

I think about that conversation a lot. Hart demonstrated what it meant to be invested in a club. It wasn't enough for him to say to Demichelis, 'Ignore the idiot on TV.' He decided to confront me, and in the process try to change things.

My respect for Hart only increased in that moment. He showed that being a leader isn't just about directing your team – it's about standing up for them when it really matters. And for my part, I never made a joke about any unlucky defender again.

NEVER LEAD ALONE

Leadership isn't what you think.

We often assume that leading is about controlling every element of an organisation. But it's not. Like Sean Dyche, leaders set a team's top-line objectives and behaviours – and trust their squad to get it right.

We're usually told that leading is about doing everything yourself. But it's not. Like Ben Francis, leaders are just as mindful of what they *shouldn't* do, and pass that responsibility on to their peers.

We might think leading is a lonely path. But it's not. Like Phil Neville, leaders find a group of cultural architects to support them, so they're never truly alone.

In all, leadership is a less demanding, punishing, and lonely path than you might think. Nobody leads in isolation. Instead, leadership spreads outwards through a whole group – in 'ripples', as Neville put it.

And that means that anyone can be a leader. Even you.

If there's one leader who represents these characteristics better than anyone, it's Kevin Sinfield, one of the most successful ever leaders of the Leeds Rhinos. In the course of over a decade at the helm, he led the Rugby League team to seven Grand Final wins, two Challenge Cups and three World Club Challenges. It's a record that makes him one of the most-awarded captains in the sport's 125-year history.

On the podcast, we asked him how he did it. His answers were a masterclass in leadership. First, he thought his job was to set the broad behaviours that the team should emulate: 'Actions speak louder than words. People want to see the behaviours – they're the things that stand out more, they're the things that carry far more weight than any dressing room team talk.'

At the same time, Sinfield knew that he could say 'no'. '[The team] were so important to me – the support they gave me, but also in allowing me to have the humility to say "You're better at this than me," or "I think your voice here would resonate far further than mine would."' It was a masterclass in cutting out the bullshit.

Above all, he depended on a wider group of cultural architects: 'I was captain of the side for thirteen years, but I had some wonderful leaders around me. Without them we wouldn't have got anywhere near what we did.'

The same three ingredients of leadership, again and again. Set behaviours. Focus on what matters. Find your lieutenants.

When you're leading a group in this way, leadership becomes a process of collaboration, not instruction. Michelle Mone, the founder of the lingerie brand Ultimo, is widely credited as one of the best businesspeople of her generation – a woman who, after being made redundant from her marketing job, built one of the most successful fashion companies of recent decades. Her business is renowned for its creativity, and the loyalty of its customers. On the podcast, she told us that true leadership isn't about setting yourself apart from your team – it's about embedding yourself with it. 'We're a team,' she told us. 'And I always treated my team with respect. I didn't ever ask them to do something if I wasn't willing to do it myself ... I suppose I was a leader like that.'

'I always treated my team with respect.
I didn't ever ask them to do something if I
wasn't willing to do it myself.' Michelle Mone

It's a lesson that reveals that leadership need not be solitary. In your high performance journey, there will be moments when you feel the pressure is too much. You'll be called upon to lead, and will think you don't have what it takes. And you'll be invited to make decisions that feel beyond you.

In such moments, recall these principles of leadership and take heart. Leading isn't about obsessively controlling everything. It isn't even always about making all the calls yourself. It's about setting direction – and trusting those around you to do the right thing.

LESSON SUMMARY

- Leaders aren't autocrats. They set the direction, and trust their teams to find the path themselves.
- What does this entail? First, leaders outline the group's objectives. Find your big, hairy, audacious goal – or BHAG – and make it central to everything you do.
- Second, leaders cut out the bullshit. A crucial part of leadership is directing people what *not* to do.
- Third, leaders never act alone. Seek out your cultural architects – the high-status, likeable, talented individuals who everyone in the group admires. And trust them.
- Remember that leadership is high-pressure, but it need never be solitary. Leaders are part of the team, not above it – and that makes leadership less scary than you might think.

If you answer
the 'why', then
the 'what' and the
'how' will soon
follow.

CRAFT A CULTURE

I n the years before Mauricio Pochettino's appointment as head coach, Tottenham were always just good enough. Usually found languishing somewhere in the middle of the Premier League, the club were rarely on the verge of relegation – but almost never in with a shot at major titles. The no-hoper culture of the club was encapsulated in a disparaging phrase Alex Ferguson used when he wanted Manchester United players to relax about facing Spurs: 'Lads, it's Tottenham.'

'The club's culture was described to me with an apt image: "All fur coat and no knickers",' Pochettino has said of the era before he joined.[1] When he arrived, his first goal was to change that.

His solution? To transform the club's culture. 'A crucial ingredient for success is a club's culture,' Pochettino told his biographer.[2] 'The ethos, the rules, deep-seated things that must be respected and serve as a yardstick.'

Within years of Pochettino's arrival, Tottenham's culture would be unrecognisable. When we sat down in his beautiful London home for his *High Performance* interview, the avuncular Argentine gradually unveiled how he had changed the mood of the dressing room. 'It's a question of two things: energy and attitude,'

Pochettino said. Whenever he felt his players were underperforming, it was down to their failure to focus on these two traits.

'Attitude is everything,' he explained. 'You can have all the talent that God provides you with, but without attitude – the ability to be open, to listen and learn – you are not going to achieve anything.'

'You can have all the talent that God provides you with, but without attitude, you won't achieve anything.' Mauricio Pochettino

And energy? 'Energía universal', the Argentinean said, slipping into Spanish. Universal energy. To Pochettino, this energy is a kind of life force – it seeps into everything. He described how he could glean his players' energy merely by shaking their hands. 'When you touch some people, you feel the energy,' he told us. 'You feel if he's good, if he needs love, if he's upset, if he slept well.' And why does this matter? 'Because you are not going to manage a road – you are going to manage a person!' 'Energía universal' might sound mystical, but its practical implications are anything but. According to Pochettino, you need to give out the kind of energy that you want to define your life. If you're needlessly pessimistic, things will go badly; if you're constantly optimistic, things will go well.

Pochettino's whole management style is focused on creating a particular culture in the club. Everyone needs to be high-energy, everyone needs to keep their mindset positive and everyone needs to feel invested in keeping up the energía universal. 'You are able to create a nice environment, a happy environment with good energy,' he said.

Pochettino's never-ending search for positive vibes led to some unusual decisions. During our discussion, he repeatedly spoke of the need to 'put our energy' into a particular player or 'give our love' to another. The best example was the case of Son Heung-min and the Asian Games. In 2018, Pochettino allowed Son to play for South Korea at the games – even though Spurs were under no obligation to release him, because they are not part of FIFA's calendar.

Why did Pochettino allow one of his most promising players to go on leave, we asked? Because it would help to maintain the positive culture in the team. The approach paid dividends. 'He is still at Tottenham because we allowed him to go and play,' said Pochettino. 'We were not selfish and saying, "No, Son needs to stay here."'

Pochettino's emphasis on culture paid off. When he arrived at Tottenham, he was charged with establishing the club in the top four. He exceeded expectations, landing the club in title contention for three successive seasons – and getting them to a historic Champions League final along the way. And it was done on the cheap, at least in Premier League terms – the result of a 'completely different project to the big sides', as Pochettino put it later.[3] Today, Pochettino is at Paris Saint-Germain, where the trend is the same. Energy and attitude take the club onwards and upwards.

In the last chapter, we examined how leadership can drive teams to be their best by offering a clear sense of direction. The trouble is, this is rarely enough to make a group thrive. As Pochettino's example shows, the best organisations don't just triumph thanks to clear leadership – they thrive because everybody feels good about the team.

Getting culture right is the last component of high performance, and it's also one of the hardest. If you want people to do their best work, you can't just tell them what to do. You need them to feel invested in the organisation – to really *want* it to succeed. If leadership is about constructing high performance teams from the top down, then culture is about building it from the bottom up.

It's a pity, then, that culture often gets forgotten. The writer David Foster Wallace once told a story about two young fish swimming in the ocean. 'They happen to meet an older fish swimming the other way, who nods at them and says, "Morning boys. How's the water?" And the two young fish swim on for a bit, and eventually one of them looks over at the other and goes, "What the hell is water?"'[4] Culture is a bit like that water. It is all around us, in everything we say, think and do. Yet all too often we don't notice it – precisely because it's everywhere.

In this chapter we uncover what a good culture looks like. And we examine how we can all build one. The answer lies in creating a sense of meaning, connection and safety – just like Pochettino's Tottenham.

THE FIVE TYPES OF CULTURE

What does a high-performing culture look like? The best answers come from Charles Duhigg's visionary book *Smarter Faster Better* – which tells the story of a pair of academics who decided to find out. In 1994, James Baron and Michael Hannan – professors at Stanford – set out to investigate what effect culture had on a company's fortunes. Based in the heart of Silicon Valley, they were in a good place to do so: Stanford was rapidly becoming a finishing school for a new generation of tech entrepreneurs. To understand the importance of a business's culture, Baron and Hannan had to do little more than leave the front gates of their university.[5]

It was surprising, then, that nobody at Stanford had ever tried to quantify the effects that culture had on a business. Sure, the odd study had tried to look into how various teams gelled together, but Baron and Hannan envisaged something more ambitious. Over the next fifteen years, they would examine the cultures of almost 200 companies, conducting surveys to investigate every possible factor that might impact a group's culture – from hiring practices and pay, to how decisions got made and why people left.

What they found amazed them.

As Duhigg recounts, the first insight was the simplest: culture mattered. A lot. Some firms thrived, others never got off the ground, yet more made it for a few years before falling victim to the dotcom boom of the early 2000s. But, in all cases, the best determinant of how a company did was its culture. The impact of cultural decisions 'is evident even after taking account of numerous other factors that might be expected to affect the success or failure of a young technology venture,' Baron and Hannan would later write.[6]

But the pair also came to realise that culture was complicated. It wasn't just a simple binary of 'good' cultures and 'bad' cultures. In fact, Duhigg describes how the professors identified five different types of culture – each with its own strengths and weaknesses.

First, there were 'star' companies. In these organisations, getting the best employees was everything. Bosses would spend lavish sums of money on recruiting the sharpest people. Once they were in, these staff would be treated like royalty: given tonnes of autonomy, hefty pay cheques and generous perks.

Second, there were the 'engineering' companies. Here, the technicians and scientists were in control. Everything was rigorous and data-driven. The people who succeeded were those with a knack for technical tasks, or who were good at thinking about the company's operations. Many software engineering companies fitted this mould.

Next up were 'bureaucracies', in which every decision was governed by rules, policies and convoluted systems. Decisions were supposed to be made by committee; in practice they frequently weren't made at all. These bureaucracies had a cousin in the fourth type of culture, 'autocracies', which were also highly convoluted and rule-bound, but in this instance all those rules were created to appease one, all-powerful figure (usually the CEO).

Finally, there was the 'commitment' model. In a commitment culture, people work at the organisation because they have a strong connection to it – they feel invested in its purpose, they care about their colleagues. These companies place staff at the heart of everything they do (most commitment cultures avoid redundancies at all costs). These businesses invested heavily in training, emphasised high levels of teamwork and organised activities to bring staff together. Here, culture was everything.

Which of these models worked the best? Unsurprisingly, the bureaucracies and autocracies tended to perform poorly – something anyone who's worked in an excessively admin-heavy company will understand. Meanwhile, the engineering model was hit and miss: for certain industries it worked, for others less so.

Then there was the star model. Sure enough, this approach produced its share of successful companies. Putting all of the most talented people in one team could yield incredible results. But this approach was high risk: companies either went on to greatness, or went bust. Why? Well, the star companies tended to be filled with big egos, whose clashing personalities became a barrier to the company's long-term stability. Fans of Real Madrid will remember the club's *galácticos* policy, in which they signed the world's best players year after year – an approach that yielded inconsistent and underwhelming results. As one Real

Madrid manager from that era declared, 'Everyone wanted to be the maître d', no one wanted to wash the plates.'[7]

The most effective way to get results, concluded Baron and Hannan, was through the commitment model. Across almost every conceivable metric, commitment cultures performed the best. 'Not one of the commitment firms we studied failed,' Duhigg quotes them as saying. '*None* of them.' Not only that, but these companies were more profitable, less bureaucratic – and had the happiest staff.[8]

How was it that a team of apparently less talented people could do better than a team of 'stars'? The answer lay in the power of commitment. In commitment cultures, everyone was on board with what the company was doing, and everyone had a shared set of values and goals. That meant everyone worked harder.

The Stanford study is not the only evidence for the power of commitment cultures. The analytics company Gallup reports that companies with engaged employees are 22 per cent more profitable than those in which employees watch the clock.[9] The effect of commitment on individual workers' quality of life is considerable too. Another study found that a 10 per cent increase in employee trust in a company's leaders had the same impact on life satisfaction as receiving a 36 per cent increase in salary.[10] The lesson is clear: if you want to build a successful organisation, you need to make your teammates care about what you're doing. A high performance team is a committed team.

ANSWER THE BIG WHY

When he was the manager of Manchester United, Alex Ferguson would often recount a story about three men who were laying bricks. Each was asked what he was doing.

The first said, 'Laying bricks.' The second said, 'Earning £10 per hour.' The third said, 'I'm building a cathedral and, one day, I'll bring my kids back here and tell them that their dad contributed to this magnificent building.'

Ferguson told his players that they could apply these three approaches to their training sessions. Why were they playing for Manchester United, he asked?

Some players might answer, 'I'm just practising.' Others might say, 'I'm earning £1,000 per hour.' The third group would say, 'I'm helping to build the best Manchester United team ever, and I'll be proud to tell my grandchildren I was part of it.'[11]

As we'll see in the rest of this this chapter, there are a number of different ways to build a commitment culture. Ferguson's lesson hints at the first. To build a sense of commitment, you need a team to be able to answer a simple question: why?

In Lesson 2, we discovered how long-term motivation comes from finding a sense of meaning – a cause that transcends just getting paid or being promoted. But this principle doesn't just apply to individuals; it applies to whole teams. Groups need to answer the 'why' question if they're going to pull together. Subconsciously, we're all constantly asking ourselves: why? What's the point of all this? In his classic study of great organisations, *Good to Great*, Jim Collins described this as the 'extra dimension' – a sense of purpose that goes beyond merely making money.[12]

One particularly fascinating study conducted by the organisational psychologist Adam Grant reveals the power of purpose in driving teams' performance.[13] In the study, a group of call centre workers were asked to call the alumni of a university. They were raising funds for its scholarship programme. Beforehand, the callers were divided into three groups. One group were given some stories to read from previous employees about the personal benefits of the job – how they developed communication skills, the ability to pitch well, and so on. The second group met some people who had received the scholarship, who explained how the money had improved their lives. The third group weren't given any information about the scholarship at all.

A month later, the researchers assessed how the three groups were performing. The people in the first group, who'd been told about the personal benefit of working in a call centre, did no better than those who hadn't been told anything about the scholarship – both groups raised about the same amount of money. But those who were reminded of the positive effect the scholarship had on *other* people brought in significantly more money.

The lesson? When a team's members know *why* they're doing something, beyond mere personal gain, they perform at a higher level.

The same dynamic is visible among our *High Performance* interviewees. Take Tracey Neville's time coaching England's national netball team, the England Roses. The twin sister of Phil Neville and the younger sister of Gary, Tracey grew up surrounded by high-performing athletes. Her story is perhaps even more remarkable. Following an international career as a netball player, she was forced into retirement by a knee injury. Yet this didn't stop her commitment to the sport. Neville went on to study sports science, set up a netball academy, and become a coach – leading the team Manchester Thunder to two Superleague titles in three years. In 2015, she became head coach of the Roses.

It was a hard gig. For decades, the Roses had been an OK but rarely world-beating team. The pattern of Commonwealth results since 2002 – fourth, bronze, bronze, fourth – indicated a ceiling to the team's ambition. Their best performance in a world cup was silver, won in 1975. 'For years, all I heard was, "We nearly won," [or] "We should have won on paper." But our team's not on paper – our team's on the court,' Neville told one interviewer.[14]

By the time Neville joined, there was a desire to change that. Neville wanted to professionalise netball, turning the Roses from a team who had to juggle their commitments alongside 'proper' jobs into a squad of paid, full-time players. Her arrival coincided with the creation of a centralised professional netball programme in Loughborough, where players would spend four days a week training together. It was the first step to building a world-beating team.

Yet transforming the Roses would take time. Neville had her eye on the Commonwealth gold medal – but a lot stood in her way. 'When you make big changes, you can get a lot of opposition,' she once said.[15] She was asking people to leave stable jobs behind and trust her – a big ask. It didn't make Neville's task easier that, within three months of taking the head coaching role, she was tasked with leading England into a world cup in Australia. While there, her father died suddenly. In difficult circumstances, the Roses achieved another run-of-the-mill third place.

Neville knew that she had to revolutionise the team's culture. And she did. By the time England travelled to Australia's Gold Coast for the Commonwealth Games in 2018, the team felt different – more energised. The Roses played seven matches in ten days and, after a nail-biting semi-final against Jamaica, found themselves in the final.

It was another heart-stopping match. After both teams scored twenty-five goals apiece in the first half, Neville's side fell 40–36 down in the final quarter. Everything seemed lost. Then, a miracle. In the closing minutes of the game, the Roses fought their way back to 51–51. Next, with seconds left on the clock, they pulled ahead. Neville recounted how it felt to watch the final winning shot swish through the net: 'When that last shot went through that goal, the athlete in me thought "This is a dream come true."' The Roses had made history. Their first-ever gold medal.

Why did Neville's team succeed where so many previous Roses teams had failed? The answer is simple: by answering the 'why' question. The women on Neville's team had given up promising careers as zoologists, lawyers and doctors – all to play for England. Neville realised that she needed to give them a sense of higher purpose – otherwise why would they turn their backs on lucrative jobs to play netball? 'At amateur level people just turn up, do it, go home, do their jobs. At professional level, people want to know why they're doing it, why they're invested in it,' Neville told us.

And so, from day one, Neville set out to offer that sense of higher purpose. Her answer was simple: netball offered the chance to represent every woman in England. 'Netball is played by every single little girl in the country,' Neville told one interviewer. 'It is the most popular female sport ... We always knew that we were playing for – and representing – every female in the country.'[16] On the podcast, Neville reiterated this point. Women athletes, she said, had often been denied the chance to play professionally:

> They always said there was no future in it – that there was more future in education, in being a doctor and being a lawyer ... I think the real tribute to our programme now is that we have doctors, we have lawyers, but we also have international world-class athletes as well. That's the first thing I really wanted to change: [to show]

that as a sport and as women we can achieve multiple dreams.

This is precisely the kind of all-consuming purpose that contributes to a winning culture, as Neville knew. 'It helped us to commit to working hard every day for three years and even in the final two [Commonwealth Games] matches, which were decided by a total of two goals,' she has said.[17] In short: purpose drives commitment.

'I wanted to show that as a sport and as women we can achieve multiple dreams.' Tracey Neville

Of course, not all teams can find a sense of purpose that's quite as lofty as the Roses'. Most of us aren't representing 50 per cent of an entire country when we go to work. But the notion of finding your purpose can be applied in all teams. In the course of our interviews, we've been able to discern several different 'whys' that drive high-performing cultures – some ambitious, some more practically minded, but all of which go beyond the mere baubles of money and success.

Ben Francis of Gymshark, for example, found purpose in his desire to build a community between his consumers – they weren't just customers, they were like-minded people, and he had the chance to connect them. Others were motivated primarily by a desire for excellence. When we asked Eddie Jones what fuelled his relentless drive, his answer was short and succinct: 'I want to coach the perfect game.' Ineos Team UK, meanwhile, set out to prove once and for all that British sailing can be world-beating. On one level, the precise nature of the purpose doesn't matter – what matters is that it's there. Give your team a sense of purpose. If you answer the 'why', then the 'what' and the 'how' will soon follow.

HIGH PERFORMANCE PIT STOP –
THE FIVE WHYS

Sakichi Toyoda, the founder of Toyota, had a simple method for getting to the heart of problems within his business. Developed in the 1930s, the method is still used by Toyota today.

The method is designed to work out the root cause of any problem. When something goes wrong, you ask 'Why?' five times in a row. Toyoda used the method to prevent mistakes, but it can also help you find out what is really driving your team.[18]

For Tracey Neville, for example, the five whys might be as follows:

Why are you coaching the England Roses? To be the best netball team they can be.

Why? To win gold in a global tournament.

Why? To show that we are the greatest netball team on the planet.

Why? To represent every female athlete in England.

Why? To inspire the next generation of female sportspeople, and show that they can achieve their dreams.

Try it with someone you know – perhaps by asking them about their work. Yes, your incessant why-ing could prove a little irritating, but you might also be surprised by what you uncover. By delving ever deeper into what is driving our behaviour, we can identify the kind of true purpose that you need to build a commitment culture.

EQ TRUMPS IQ

'On the field today, all it will be between you is a look. No words, just a look. That will say everything.' It was King's Park, Durban, South Africa, June 1997, and Ian McGeechan was speaking to his squad, the British & Irish Lions, moments ahead of their test against South Africa. He asked them to look to the future. 'You'll meet each other in the street in thirty years' time, and there'll just be that look, and you'll know just how special some days in your life are.'[19]

In the world of rugby, McGeechan's pep talks have become famous – and with good reason. Many players have worn the Lions jersey with pride, but McGeechan embodies the spirit of the team more than anyone else.

The Scotsman's relationship with the Lions began as a player, on tours in 1974 and 1977 – tasting victory in South Africa and defeat in New Zealand. He retired from international rugby in 1979 but continued as a coach, starting out as an assistant on the Scotland coach staff. In 1989, he coached the Lions for the first time on their tour of Australia, taking the team from a disappointing first Test match to a dazzling series win.

But his whole career was building up to that moment in 1997. The Lions were the overwhelming underdogs. Yet in the wake of McGeechan's speech – his emphasis on 'that look' – the team pulled off something extraordinary. They became only the third touring side to ever win a test series in South Africa, securing a 2–1 victory against all odds.

When we brought McGeechan on to the *High Performance* podcast, he told us that the speech came from the heart. 'I had experienced that look when I was playing,' he told us. 'A simple look into the eyes of a teammate, knowing that you respect them, you understand what they have invested to be there, letting them know you have their back, is a powerful feeling.'

'A simple look into the eyes of a teammate, letting them know you have their back, is a powerful feeling.' Ian McGeechan

McGeechan's insight hints at the second key way to build a commitment culture: through the power of emotional connection.

To understand the power of these connections, it's worth looking at a fascinating study from Carnegie Mellon and MIT universities.[20] A group of psychologists set out to assess how emotional bonds within a team affect its performance. To do so, they organised a huge study involving 699 people divided into 152 teams.

Each team was given a series of challenges that depended on effective cooperation. One task involved collating a series of complicated, contradictory shopping lists into one list; another involved brainstorming ways to use a brick (you got a point for each unique idea). Faced with this bamboozling array of tasks, some teams gelled together well while others went to pieces.

More surprising was what made a team likely to succeed. Intelligence, the researchers found, counted for little. The researchers had tested their subjects' IQ beforehand, and the intellect of a team made no difference to its outcomes. But there were a few characteristics that *did* mark out the highest-performing teams.

For one thing, everyone in the best teams spoke about the same amount. Yes, in some tasks one or two team members would take the lead, but across the whole day of tests, everybody talked as much as each other. For another, the highest-performing teams were found to have 'high average social sensitivity' – they had a knack for identifying how teammates were feeling, and responding appropriately. (The academics had tested this by giving all the participants several photos of stranger's eyes, and seeing how good they were at working out their moods.)[21] All in all, the best groups were those with high levels of emotional insight into one another.

Researchers refer to this knack as 'emotional intelligence', or EQ – emotional quotient. It refers to the ability of a group to read one another's emotions, implicitly and unthinkingly – just like the 'look' that McGeechan described.

It seems that when members of a team understand each other's emotions, they work together better. They know how to cooperate. They feel more motivated. They remain more committed to the culture in the long term.

The question, then, is simple: how can you boost a team's emotional intelligence?

This might sound like a fool's errand. We all know how hard it is to boost your IQ. Why should it be any easier to boost EQ? But the science is clear. Emotional intelligence is never fixed. In the words of Travis Bradberry, the author of the bestseller *Emotional Intelligence 2.0*, emotional intelligence is 'highly malleable'. 'As you train your brain by repeatedly practising new emotionally intelligent behaviours, it builds the pathways needed to make them into habits,' he says. The very act of behaving in an emotionally intelligent way boosts your emotional intelligence.[22]

We can see this process in action by returning to the success of Kevin Sinfield, former captain of the Leeds Rhinos and one of our most thought-provoking *High Performance* interviewees. Sinfield had a stronger emotional connection to his team than most: he joined Rhinos at the age of thirteen, made his senior debut at sixteen, and became captain when still just twenty-two. But the club he took over was not in a good place: when he became captain, it had been over three decades since Leeds had won a league championship. During Sinfield's time, that picture changed dramatically. Under his leadership, the Rhinos would win the league seven times in twelve years, becoming the most successful rugby league side in two decades.

This was a puzzle. On paper, the club was never the best-resourced or most talented. Sinfield wasn't the strongest or most skilled player on the pitch, even by his own admission. England coach Steve McNamara once said that 'if Sinfield knew that he wouldn't be the best player on the park, he'd make sure he was the most prepared'.[23]

So, what led to the Rhinos' success? The answer lay in the team's commitment culture. Sinfield has always said that his greatest commitment is to his teammates: 'I always felt my job was to help people be better than they believe,' he told us.

 'I always felt my job was to help people be better than they believe.'
Kevin Sinfield

In particular, Sinfield had a knack for boosting the team's collective emotional intelligence. 'It was purely down to our culture,' Sinfield recounts. 'We were prepared to play for each other, we felt safe with and trusted one another, and we believed in what we were doing. We quickly realised we were on to something special with the brilliant group we had.'

What was most striking in our interviews, however, was that this emotional connection hadn't come naturally. It was something that had been built – crafted through deliberate choices made by Sinfield. They are choices that anyone who is a member of a team can learn from.

For one thing, Sinfield always treated his colleagues with kindness and consideration. 'Kevin never once shouted at me,' his teammate Gareth Ellis told us. 'If I wasn't trying hard enough, he would simply give me a look and that was enough. He helped create a culture where you didn't want to let each other down.'[24] This caring, affectionate attitude reached its peak when Sinfield's teammate, Rob Burrow, was diagnosed with motor neurone disease. Sinfield wanted the club to do everything it could to help his friend. 'I'd absolutely do anything for him,' Sinfield said on the podcast. And so he went to unimaginable lengths to help his friend – running a dazzling seven marathons in seven days to raise awareness about Burrow's illness.

Why did he do it? Because of his connection with his colleagues. 'I've been fortunate to play in a number of different championship-winning sides,' Sinfield said. 'But the friendships and the memories are what's important to me now.'

For another thing, Sinfield made sure to speak to everyone at Leeds Rhinos regularly – from the team assistants to the manager. Consider the words of the groundsman Jason Booth: 'He knows the name of everyone who works at the club,' he said to us. 'Whatever your job or position, he will come and chat and he always thanks you for your help and contribution. He sees it as his job to make everyone feel special.'[25] For Sinfield, knowing his colleagues well – their kids' names, their birthdays, where they'd been on holiday – was an integral part of building a sense of connection.

Sinfield's example shows that emotional intelligence is simple to master. Simple, but not easy: it requires long-term, consistent effort. If you want to build your EQ, then memorise people's names and the names of their families and kids. Make sure you're giving everybody in your team the chance to speak. Actively study the emotional reactions of every member of the team, however junior. Does everyone seem comfortable? Is there any habit of the group that seems to make some members upset? The goal is for an unusually strong emotional connection between everyone in the team.

With time, everyone will learn to read a 'look' as effectively as Ian McGeechan.

HIGH PERFORMANCE PIT STOP –
PEOPLE FIRST

Damian

I once spent a day with Angelo Dundee, the legendary boxing trainer. By the time I met him, Dundee had worked with over a dozen world boxing champions – most notably supporting Muhammad Ali from the corner of the ring during his most iconic fights, including the 'Rumble in the Jungle' and the 'Thrilla in Manila'.

I was like a kid in a sweetshop, eager to hear Dundee's anecdotes and get to grips with his philosophy. 'What was this fighter *really* like?' 'How did that fighter deal with *that*?' 'What did you say to *that* fighter?' For an hour or so, Dundee was characteristically kind and indulged my curiosity. But eventually my questions wore a little thin – and Dundee took the opportunity to teach me a simple but powerful lesson.

'Damian,' he said, 'I think you may have misunderstood my work. I don't work with fighters.'

There was a moment of confusion. I was pretty sure that he did, actually. I felt a look of confusion and embarrassment creeping on to my face. Then Dundee continued: 'I don't work with fighters. I work with young men who happen to fight for a living.'

After the interview had ended, I spent a long time reflecting on Dundee's words. What had he meant? With time, I came to realise what he was getting at. These boxing legends weren't, in the first instance, boxers – they were people, with loves and hates, ambitions and disappointments. And being their trainer was about realising that they were people first, fighters second.

It was a powerful insight into the importance of emotional intelligence. Today, I know that building a high-performing team is all about understanding your peers as individuals. Think about their emotions, ask about their families, reflect on what they're thinking. They are people first, potential high performers second.

MAKE PEOPLE FEEL SAFE

Amy Edmondson, an organisational psychologist at Harvard Business School, has spent her career studying the science of good teams. Her interest began in the early 1990s. Early in her academic career, another professor asked Edmondson to help her examine why medical mistakes came about, and so she began documenting the number of errors taking place in hospitals in Boston – visiting wards, speaking to doctors and nurses and closely observing how things ticked.[26]

The first thing that Edmondson noticed was the scary number of errors in every hospital, every day. 'You would be shocked at how many mistakes occur every day,' she later said – not because of incompetence, but because hospitals are really complicated places. 'There's a lot of opportunities for something to slip through the cracks,' she told Charles Duhigg, who recounts the whole story vividly in *Smarter Faster Better*.[27] Some of the slip-ups were scary: Edmondson witnessed a nurse accidentally give a patient an anaesthetic instead of a blood thinner; another patient, she noticed, had been given amphetamines rather than aspirin. Some errors, Edmondson came to realise, were fairly inevitable; but clearly some wards were more error-prone than others.

Edmondson came up with a hypothesis: perhaps, she thought, the teams that gelled best were less likely to make mistakes. And so she conducted an experiment. Edmondson and her team created a questionnaire to measure how well a team in any given ward worked together. The results were bizarre. When she collated the data, Edmondson found that the wards where the teams worked together well made far *more* mistakes. She was bewildered. How could the most cohesive teams end up with the worst results?

After pouring over the data for several weeks, Edmondson had a brainwave. To test out her new theory, she asked nurses on the wards a different question: 'If you make a mistake, is it held against you?' Here, too, there were a wide array of responses – in some wards, everyone seemed to be holding a dizzying array of grudges; in others, mistakes were instantly forgiven. But this time, the answers made more sense. Where people felt their colleagues were holding grudges, fewer mistakes were reported; where people felt they had permission to make errors, more mistakes made it into the records. As Duhigg later summarised it, 'It wasn't that strong teams made more mistakes. Rather, it was that those who belonged to strong teams felt more comfortable *admitting* their mistakes.'[28]

Therein were the origins of Edmondson's most important idea – one that has transformed sports teams and companies around the world. She called it 'psychological safety'.

Imagine a workplace where you hold back from asking questions or sharing ideas, because of the fear of seeming incompetent. You can never really be yourself, and you can never really relax. This is a workplace with a sense of psychological danger – you are constantly on edge. Now, imagine a workplace in which everyone is safe to take risks, offer their views, ask daft questions and admit their failures. You can let your guard down, knowing you won't be laughed at or sacked. This workplace offers psychological safety.

According to Edmondson, in psychologically safe environments, there is a 'shared belief, held by members of a team, that the group is a safe place for taking risks'. The goal, according to Edmondson, is to create 'a sense of confidence that the team will not embarrass, reject or punish someone for speaking up'.[29] You can admit to errors and acknowledge failure, knowing that you won't be judged or disciplined.

Since Edmondson began her research, psychological safety has become one of the most influential ideas in global management.[30] Most famously, Google once ran an enormous study of 180 teams, analysing over 250 different team attributes – and found that psychological safety correlates strongly with the best-performing teams.[31]

The trouble is, in our day-to-day lives there are dozens of pressures that discourage us from building psychological safety into our teams. In the short term, focusing on behaviours that create trust can be arduous. If you're a manager, it's usually easier to cut off a junior employee so you can reach a decision quickly, or to express frustration about an obvious mistake that affects your company's bottom line. Eventually, however, these small actions can have a corrosive effect on psychological safety.

How can we prevent this tendency undermining our teams? On the *High Performance* podcast, some of the best insights came from Tracey Neville. Ever the model of a commitment culture, the England Roses encapsulate the power of psychological safety better than anyone.

Neville was unequivocal about how she altered the team's atmosphere. 'It wasn't a happy place when I arrived,' she recounted. 'We had to change the mentality.' This is something that one of your authors, Damian, witnessed first-hand, when working as a coaching consultant to the team. During her first few months, Neville remained focused on one thing: building the kind of environment she had thrived in when she was a player. We kept returning to the fact that the best cultures made people feel safe, valued and respected.

And so Neville set about making people feel safe. 'My first idea was to invest a lot of time in team bonding,' she said to us:

At Manchester Thunder I had the time to develop relationships with my players and create feelings of trust and loyalty. When I was appointed national coach, we did different things that gave them lots of social interaction and with lots of laughs. This helped to break down any barriers.

The goal here was to build such a sense of trust between players that they could be honest and open with each other – just as Edmondson had called for. As Ama Agbeze, the Roses captain, once put it: 'We work well together off the court. We both have faith in each other.'[32] Neville's experience shows that, once there is a sense of trust, everything else becomes easier.

Second, Neville wanted her team to feel comfortable failing in front of one another. 'If we wanted to win, we had to do things differently,' she told us. 'We had to get used to failing, failing fast and getting better.' This was a point that she kept emphasising during the training: 'I give them permission to try my way and accept they may sometimes get it wrong.' 'Getting it wrong,' she continued, 'is just another way of learning.'

 'If we wanted to win, we had to get used to failing, failing fast and getting better.' Tracey Neville

In practice, this meant arranging activities that took the players out of their comfort zone and got them used to making errors. On one occasion, she invited the England Lionesses football team – who were being managed by her twin brother Phil – to train alongside their netball counterparts. They played a series of competitive games, including one where they swapped sports, with the Lionesses playing netball and the Roses playing football.

The result was a safe, trusting and caring environment. Everyone had failed in front of each other before, and so they felt able to push themselves – maybe even fail – again. In our interview, Neville told us how close she had become to her Roses team by the time they won the 2018 Commonwealth Games. 'Sometimes it was the team who made you wake up every day and get back on with it,' she said. 'They became your family, so you felt like you could achieve anything with that group of players.'

Neville's approach chimes with that of the other high performance cultures we've met in this chapter. From Tottenham Hotspur to Leeds Rhinos, the successful teams foster a sense of trust and openness – a culture in which people can be frank about their weaknesses, even their failures. Psychological safety gets the goods.

HIGH PERFORMANCE PIT STOP – SAFETY NET

Damian

When I was working with Tracey Neville and the England Roses, the pair of us used a simple exercise to work out how psychologically safe the culture was. Every four weeks, we would ask the players to answer the following questions – which we borrowed from one of Amy Edmondson's seminal papers on psychological safety.[33]

1. *If I make a mistake on my team, do I feel it's held against me?*

2. *Are my colleagues able to bring up problems and tough issues?*

3. *Is it safe to take a risk?*

4. *Is it difficult to ask other members of this team for help?*

5. *When I am working with colleagues, do I feel my unique skills and talents are valued and used?*

This exercise served as a handy checklist throughout the journey to that Commonwealth Games gold. But you can use it too. Try asking these questions about your own working life – or even asking them of your team. How psychologically safe is your environment? And what could you do to build the sense of safety in each area?

CULTURE IS PEOPLE

'We talk a lot about culture in every business, in every sport,' said Gareth Southgate. 'Culture is created by people.'

It was a few weeks before the European Football Championships in 2021, and England's manager was telling us about the importance of culture. Of all of our high performers, Southgate's insights were perhaps the most intriguing. Here was a man who had taken over the England role when the team were at their lowest ebb. They were seen as a national embarrassment, fresh from a humiliating defeat to Iceland in 2016 – topped off by Sam Allardyce's appointment to the top job, and subsequent dismissal after just one game. The Three Lions were on the ropes.

In the years that followed, England transformed. In 2021, Southgate was elevated into the company of another national treasure, Alf Ramsey, by becoming only the second man to take England to the semi-finals of two successive tournaments. By the time Southgate took the Three Lions to their first final in an international tournament since the World Cup in 1966, excitement in England had reached a fever pitch. Although they would lose to Italy on penalties in the final, everyone could agree: this England team was different.

How had Southgate done it? We might put it down to two words: commitment culture. When we asked him what kind of atmosphere had had hoped to build at England, he gave an answer that was almost a word-for-word definition. 'I want them to enjoy it … Wanting to be there, wanting to be part of something that they feel is high level, is enjoyable, that culturally is right – I think that is very important to people.'

But he also told us something striking. It's about 'having the right people in the building,' he said. Why? Because 'culture is created by people'.

This raised an interesting tension, we thought. If culture is 'created by people', how can leaders create it from the top down? After all, Southgate wasn't one to shy from leadership. 'I recognise that people have to be led, and people have to be guided, and they look to the leader for answers, particularly in moments of pressure,' he said. 'But everybody is responsible for creating the environment.'

'People have to be led. But everybody
is responsible for creating the
environment.' Gareth Southgate

So what *is* the role of leaders in building a culture? The answer, Southgate suggested, is to lead by example. 'It's what you do every day,' he said. 'I can talk to the players about how I want things to be. If I then stand on the sideline and my behaviours are completely different to that … They're not going think that it's OK to make a mistake or to play without fear.'

Southgate's insight is the final ingredient in making a high performance team. Culture is created by everyone, collectively. But that doesn't mean that leaders can abdicate responsibility. It is the job of leaders to set an example – so that their team can feel truly at home.

It's not just the England football team. Think of Tracey Neville, who forged the culture of the Roses by her actions – showing them it was OK to be open, even to fail.

Or think of Kevin Sinfield, speaking to every single employee of Leeds Rhinos – and demonstrating to his team what a good culture felt like.

Or think of Mauricio Pochettino, shaking hands with each of his players – all to reveal the power of 'energía universal' to his young team.

Bas ter Weel, an economist who has studied the internal dynamics of football teams, compared managers' influence to that of prime ministers on the economy: although it is marginal, no other single individual has more influence.[34] This is a little like the role of individuals in forging a culture.

Leaders can't create a culture alone. After all, culture is people.

But leaders can set an example. They can show their teams what a positive atmosphere would look like. If culture is in anyone's hands, it's theirs.

LESSON SUMMARY

- Culture is everywhere. But we often ignore it. This is a mistake – because if you can forge a high-engagement 'commitment culture', high performance takes care of itself.
- Three ingredients make a commitment culture. First, meaning. People need a sense of purpose. Try to answer that simple, all-important question: why are we doing this?
- Second, connection. Attempt to boost the emotional bonds within a group. Take stock frequently: are your teammates happy or sad, motivated or demoralised?
- Third, safety. Team members must feel able to make mistakes. Don't hold grudges and learn to embrace failure.
- Remember Gareth Southgate's rule: 'Culture is created by people.' And that means it's everyone's responsibility – from assistant to manager, secretary to CEO.

High performance is never about lying to yourself. It is about becoming yourself.

THE COURAGE TO PERFORM

We were sitting in a boardroom inside the sleek Red Bull Formula 1 racing office in Milton Keynes. All around us were reminders of the team's success: four world championship trophies took pride of place in the cabinets, and a six-foot print of Red Bull's race-winning car loomed above us. And before us was the man who had made it all happen: team principal Christian Horner. We had asked him our classic question: what does high performance mean to you?

Horner embraced the question with gusto. Even by the standards of our most ambitious interviewees, his answer was wide-ranging:

> Ultimately, it's the car. But it's also generating and focusing your performance into all aspects that contribute to that. It's getting the most out of people – being the best that you can be. It's understanding where your weaknesses are, understanding where your strengths are. It encompasses all aspects of competition, and of life.

In other words, it was everything.

At the beginning of this book, we compared high performance to an F1 race. High performance emerges from countless small components working together – motor and chassis, engineer and driver, mind and body, individual and team. The highest-performing people operate like a well-oiled machine: every twist of a bolt, every splash of oil, every push on the accelerator comes together to drive them forward.

'High performance encompasses all aspects of competition, and of life.' Christian Horner

As Horner might put it: high performance is about the car, but it's about everything that contributes to the car too.

By now, we hope you've seen what happens when the car is running smoothly. The first step is a high performance mindset. Think of it as the car's engine. It will give you the horsepower to speed along the road of high performance. But it's not simple. Like an F1 engine, a high performance mindset requires clever engineering and constant check-ups.

That process has three steps. Everything starts with taking responsibility for your actions. What happens may not be your fault. Often it isn't – all of our lives are defined by forces beyond our control – but it is your responsibility to deal with what happens in the most effective way. The goal is what psychologists call 'high self-efficacy' – a sense that what happens to you is in your hands alone. Remember the words of Robin van Persie: 'Losers look at who to blame, and who to point the finger at. Winners point the finger at themselves.'

Next, there's motivation. High performers are rarely driven by external trinkets, whether that's a pay rise or a promotion. Instead, their motivation comes from within. Bear in mind the insights of self-determination theory, which demonstrates that the most motivated people are those who are driven by the inherent fulfilment of a task. Fortunately enough, this internal motivation is something we can all engineer. As Zack George, Britain's fittest man, told us, 'Motivation is a choice, not something that simply happens to you.'

And then there are your emotions. This isn't a book that wants anyone to suppress their emotions, or to bottle them up. But there are ways to respond healthily to the negative emotions that affect us all: anxiety, stress, despair. The trick lies in getting your 'red brain' under control, so that you can think calmly under pressure. We can all take a step back from the problems we're facing by asking ourselves three questions: what is actually being demanded of me here? What abilities do I have that can help me deal with this problem? What is really at stake?

But that's only the car's engine. The second component of your high-performing vehicle is behaviour. Think of it as the car's chassis. If the engine is powering the car, the chassis allows it to move along the track. This is what high performance behaviours offer: they let you move forward in your life, rather than remaining stranded where you are.

The journey to high performance behaviour also has three steps. First, you need to play to your strengths. High performers know that obsessing over our weaknesses can be toxic. Instead, they identify their unique skills – and play up to them. But how? Well, it begins with vigilance. Keep your eye out for moments in which you seem to be excelling, and consider why. In particular, remember the three Rs: recognition, reflection and rhythm. Are there moments where others have recognised your strengths, and told you about them? When you reflect on your past successes, are there a handful of skills that unite them? And are there any tasks that you find yourself completely lost in, the rhythm of the work being all you need to sustain you?

Once you've found your strengths, you can set off towards a life that uses them to your advantage. But even a well-chosen road won't always be a smooth one. You need to be able to overcome any obstacles that you face – and you can do so by getting a flexible perspective. Our high performers have a knack for responding creatively to their thorniest problems. They do so by boosting their self-belief, and by getting outside of themselves – learning to see their problems from a fresh perspective, and even asking for others' help in solving them. The power of flexible thinking was summarised by record-breaking Olympian Ben Ainslie: 'When the world zigs, I tend to zag.'

But it's not enough to be creative sometimes. It's not even enough to be creative most of the time. The most impressive people are all about consistency: turning one-off behaviours into long-term habits. To do so, they harness the power of trademark behaviours. These are the non-negotiable, consistent actions that will drive you to success. For Clive Woodward's England rugby team, that meant not just being on time, but being early. For Alex Ferguson's Manchester United, that meant dressing smartly. Whatever they pick, all high-performing individuals identify a handful of non-negotiables – and stick to them. These habits can be transformative. As Woodward told us, 'If you are good, you'll get there. If you are consistent, you'll stay there.'

Anyone who's watched an F1 race, however, will know that the car isn't everything. Races are won or lost by the support team: the team principal, the engineers, the behind-the-scenes tacticians. When a car pulls into the pit stop, dozens of people descend on it to change the tyres and lubricate its wheels. You also need a high-performing team to win your race.

How? Well, it's in each of our hands to lead the people around us. Good leaders, though, aren't dictators. They don't micro-manage, and they don't have to. In many respects, true leadership is hands-off. It's about setting audacious targets, and trusting your team to achieve them. And it's about finding the natural lieutenants around you – the 'cultural architects' – who can forge a high performance atmosphere.

Which leads us to culture. Success comes not just from the top down, but from the bottom up. You need everyone in the team to feel committed to the group's objectives. And so the final step to high performance is about building a 'commitment culture': making it clear to your team why they should care about the group and creating a safe, nurturing environment in which they can be themselves. As Tracey Neville put it, 'People want to know why they're doing it.' Answer that question, and a vibrant culture will follow.

 'At amateur level people just turn up. At professional level, people want to know why they're doing it.' Tracey Neville

Engine, chassis, support staff. Mindset, behaviour, team. But you might be wondering, *Where's the driver in all of this?* The answer is simple.

That's you.

Only you can set the direction of the car.

Only you can take your vehicle around the sharpest corners.

Only you can accelerate down the home straight.

Many people will help you in your journey to high performance. But you're the one behind the steering wheel.

THE CALL OF COURAGE

But there's something missing. A final characteristic that lurked, quiet and unassuming, in the background of every single one of our podcast interviews. One that many of our high performers were too modest to even mention.

Courage.

It's courage that got Billy Monger back behind the wheel of his racing car just months after losing his legs.

It's courage that made Kelly Holmes push herself to win gold in Athens in 2004, even when everyone told her that she was too old.

It's courage that convinced Gareth Southgate he could transform a demoralised England team, daring to rebuild their culture from the ground up.

In your high performance journey, you'll need to be courageous too. The road to high performance is daunting. By definition, it involves moving away from the ordinary: that mindset you've been falling back on for years, those behaviours that make up your everyday routine, the way you approach your relationships – not just with your colleagues, but with your friends and family too.

Becoming a high performer requires change. And change is scary. You need to be brave.

Yet all too often, courage gets forgotten. In the course of researching *High Performance*, we came across dozens of books on managing risk and hedging your bets. We came across all too few on the power of bravery. It's like going into a bookshop to buy *The Joy of Sex* and being told that there are no books about sex, but over twenty different books on reducing impotence. While courage is no guarantee of success, it is almost impossible to be successful without it.

And so we've chosen to end this book with a tribute to courage. But what actually *is* courage? At first glance, the answer seems simple. It's about never feeling scared – even when you're facing the most intimidating of situations. Isn't it? After all, if someone like Ant Middleton felt fear in the way the rest of us do, there's no way he could have led missions against the Taliban. If Tracey Neville was easily intimidated, how could she go from a career-ending injury to revolutionising the England Roses' performance?

Yet it's a lie. High performers do feel fear. Often, they feel it even more intensely than the rest of us.

Consider Jonny Wilkinson's description of how he viewed rugby early in his career, before he went on his journey of self-discovery. In the build-up to games, he'd experience 'just a crippling fear that what I was about to go through, or what I'd already been through, would define me'.

Or take Tom Daley's description of entering a growth spurt during his teenage years and suddenly losing the ability to dive: 'I remember I hit my feet on the board, I hit my head on the board. I landed flat so many times that it got to a point where I was like, *I'm terrified. I can't go up there anymore.*' Eventually, he developed a fear of the diving board: 'I was like, *I have no idea how to do this. I'm too terrified to even jump.* Something that I'd done for so many years, I am too scared to go.'

Or consider Kelly Jones' description of his struggle with fear throughout his career: 'We're all scared of stuff, we're all terrified of being here ... You can pick a million issues but it all comes back to the same basis really: fear.'

These people are high performers. They're emblems of courage. And yet they've all experienced fear – sometimes extreme fear. Their stories indicate that courage isn't what it seems. Real courage isn't about supressing fear, or avoiding it altogether.

Courage is about feeling fear, embracing it and finding a way to thrive anyway.

 'It's unrealistic to say to any sportsperson, "Play without fear". That's the hardest thing to do.' Gareth Southgate

Gareth Southgate put it most simply. 'It's unrealistic to say to any sportsperson, "Play without fear". I mean, what is that? It's a nonsense, because it's the hardest thing to do,' he told us. 'It's making sure that we're not consumed by that, and making sure that it's not inhibiting us.'

We need a new way of thinking about courage.

BEYOND FEAR

So, how can we build true courage? The kind of courage that doesn't involve supressing our fear, but embracing it?

We've asked dozens of high performers about overcoming fear. Their answers have been wide-ranging. Josh Warrington, the world champion boxer, told us that fear was like a fire. It could consume you or it could warm you, depending on how you responded. The racing driver Jenson Button explained to us that only when he had learned to verbalise his fear could he feel released from its grip. Not On The High Street's Holly Tucker told us about her ambiguous relationship with fear: even though she often feels like an imposter, she told us she's 'not scared about failing' because she is always looking to the future.

Between them, these high performers have offered us a toolkit for building true courage. The same solutions come through again and again – and they're solutions we can all use.

First, ask for help. Throughout this book, we've seen time and again that the road to high performance can be lonely. And time and again, we've seen that the solution lies in leaning on the people we trust. We've seen how, when Ben Francis felt that his responsibilities as CEO of Gymshark were too much, he turned to his colleagues – knowing they could take on the responsibilities that he couldn't. And we've seen how, when he was captain of Leeds Rhinos, Kevin Sinfield took the pressure off by asking for support from his squad: 'You're better at this than me,' or 'I think your voice here would resonate far further than mine would,' he would say.

When you have people around you whom you trust, the burden of high performance becomes lighter. The fear is shared. And, suddenly, courage becomes possible.

Matthew McConaughey, the Hollywood actor, made this point to us more powerfully than anyone. Here was a man whose career had been defined by dizzying highs and terrifying lows, from being derided as 'the romcom guy, the shirtless guy on the beach,' as he told us, to becoming one of the best-regarded actors of his generation, winning an Oscar for his performance in *Dallas Buyers Club*. How had he remained courageous through it all, we'd wondered. The answer lay in his relationships – and particularly his commitment to his family:

It's a gift to find things in life that we can be committed to. It gives us a compass, an anchor in this world. My family's non-negotiable, me as a father, non-negotiable, as a husband, non-negotiable. Boy, to have those and go: 'Well, whenever nothing else makes sense in the world, I got that.' I know if I can go to that, I can't go wrong – and I have more courage to go out further and try out different things.

But, by itself, the support of others isn't enough. We also need to believe in ourselves. And this leads to our second principle of building courage: remember how far you've come. Your journey to high performance will be long. There will be setbacks. And, in these moments, it will become all too easy to forget how much you've achieved. This book has described Kelly Holmes, alone in a hotel room in France, feeling that she was a failure – at a point when she was one of the fastest women in the world. It has recounted Robin van Persie sledging himself, convincing himself he had no control of his life – even though he was one of the most promising young players in Arsenal's history.

'It's a gift to find things in life that we can be committed to. It gives us a compass.' Matthew McConaughey

When fear becomes all-consuming, try looking back on what you *have* achieved. You have it in you to be whoever you want to be – you just need to remind yourself of the skills you do have.

Remember how Dina Asher-Smith dealt with her fear of failure during the 2019 World Athletics Championships? After an initial slow start, she started to panic. As she got more and more stressed about her performance, her coach John Blackie reminded her of all that she had achieved already: 'You're just going to go out there next time and do your normal start.

That's all you do.' As Asher-Smith put it, Blackie's genius was in 'affirming that what you already have within you is what you need to do to win'. And win she did. We can all heed this lesson. Keep in mind what you've achieved already. You might be further along the journey to high performance than you think.

And yet, if you do still fail, how should you react? How can you feel brave when everything really *is* going wrong? Herein lies the power of our third insight into courage: don't fear failure, celebrate it.

You see, failure is inevitable. In this book you've read about Manchester United manager Ole Gunnar Solskjær's disastrous attempt to lead Cardiff City, culminating in the worst season for the club in years. You've heard about Rio Ferdinand's form slipping in the late 1990s, leading to the greatest disappointment of his life – being missed out of the England squad in 2000. And if you hark all the way back to the book's introduction you'll recall one of your authors just about failing his A-Levels.

All of us experience failure. And failure is scary. It makes us want to give up.

But we've also seen that failure isn't something to be afraid of. If we never failed, that would mean we'd never tried. Failure can even be useful – it's the quickest way to work out what *not* to do, after all. You might recall Tracey Neville's mantra from the England Roses: 'We had to get used to failing, failing fast and getting better.'

True courage, then, is about looking failure in the eye and pushing through it. It's about knowing that failure isn't something to be afraid of. And it's about not holding a grudge when those around you fail, because you know that failure is the fuel of high performance.

When the legendary Liverpool player Steven Gerrard came on the podcast, he was unequivocal about the power of failure. 'I think sometimes failure helps you to become better,' he told us. 'Analyse, reflect, work out how and why – and go again.' This isn't to deny the hold that failure has over us. 'It's horrible, but it's happened,' as Gerrard put it. Eventually, failure becomes something everyday.

 'Failure helps you to become better. Analyse, reflect, work out how and why – and go again.' Steven Gerrard

Perhaps we can't eradicate our fear of failing. But we can look failure in the eye, and embrace it. That's real courage.

AUTHENTIC PERFORMANCE

'When I was captain at Crystal Palace at the age of twenty-three, I wanted to be the first in the running, and the last in the bar. I felt I had to achieve all of those things to be able to lead.'

Gareth Southgate was telling us about his first taste of leadership. Unexpectedly early in his career, he had found himself at the helm of Crystal Palace – and felt the pressure was on to be the kind of dominant player his team would admire.

Yet, thirty years later, the man before us has become renowned for his understated style of leadership – his kindness, humility and quietness. It was an approach that has won the affection of the England team and of a generation of fans. Within weeks of our interview, this style would take England to its best performance in a major tournament in over half a century.

What had happened to the younger, brasher Southgate, we wondered? As Southgate put it, he had realised that leaders don't need to be the 'alpha male'. 'People might think, because I appear a bit calmer, a little bit more thoughtful, that I don't care as much, or I'm not as passionate about it,' he told us. 'It's a driver for me to prove to people that [leadership] does stir me, that there's another way.'

The key to his success, Southgate told us, was simple: authenticity. 'I think our league is rich with some of the best coaches in the world. They've all got different ways but they've got to be themselves – it's got to be the way that's authentic to them,' he said. 'People smell it a mile off, if you're not yourself.'

In this moment, Southgate alluded to the final component of real courage. Each of us is constantly surrounded by people telling us what we should do, who we should be. Often, this advice can be alluring – it points us towards the 'right thing to do'. Matthew McConaughey spent much of his career getting jobs in romcoms: it seemed like the right thing to do. Ole Gunnar Solskjær took on the management of Cardiff City: it seemed like the right thing to do. Gareth Southgate became the alpha male at Crystal Palace: it seemed like the right thing to do.

But all these people eventually came to realise their mistake. Real courage isn't about doing what you're told is a good idea – it's about doing what's right for you. As McConaughey told us, you can gain a lot from following the rule, 'Do unto others what you would have them do unto you.' But you shouldn't let it distract you from the underlying truth: 'Not everyone wants to do what you want to do.'

Courage – real courage – is about finding a path that's true to you. As this book has shown, there's no single way to be a high performer. You could be a Hollywood A-lister, a sporting hero or a business leader. Or you could be a teacher, a personal assistant or, like us, two dads from Norwich and Manchester. High performance depends on each of our circumstances, interests and ambitions.

And that is why high performance is so freeing. Sure, many high-performing people share a few traits. This book has tried to uncover them. But, at heart, high performance means living a life that's authentic. It's about working out what matters to you – and pursuing it above all else.

High performance is never about lying to yourself. It is about becoming yourself. And it's about enjoying the journey. As Matthew McConaughey told us, 'Life is a verb. Go and live it.'

ACKNOWLEDGEMENTS

JAKE

I would like to thank a few key people for helping to create *High Performance*. First of all, my mum and dad, who gave me the two most important things you can give a child: roots and wings. I rely on you both every single day.

Thanks must also go to Fearne Cotton, creator of the amazing *Happy Place* podcast. You were the first person I called when I had the idea for *High Performance*. At that time I felt the podcast market was saturated, and that we'd struggle to make an impact – your passion made me think otherwise.

Of course, *High Performance* – both the podcast and especially this book – owes a great debt of thanks to the professor, Damian Hughes. You bring warmth, empathy, knowledge and awesome questions to every episode.

And finally the biggest thank yous go to my children, Flo and Seb, and my awesome wife, Harriet. Every day, just being around you gives me the energy, direction, passion and drive I need to keep on pushing myself. You are the three greatest things in my life.

DAMIAN

I have spent a large part of my life immersed within high-performing cultures. I would like to extend my appreciation and gratitude to the people who have helped guide me in my journey to understand them.

Thank you Geraldine for your rich love, deep wisdom, gentle humour, enthusiastic support, bottomless patience and generous friendship. I love you more than I can express in words.

George and Rose, this book – along with everything else I do – is for you. Thank you for blessing me with your love, laughter, curiosity, kindness, understanding and all-round brilliance. I hope this book shows how you can combine decency, humility and hard work and still flourish at whatever you choose to do. Keep shining brightly. I love you both.

Thank you to my brilliantly supportive parents, Brian and Rosemarie, my dear brothers, Anthony and Chris, and my sister, Rachael. Your example, encouragement, interest and unfailing friendship are a source of endless comfort.

I owe a huge debt of gratitude to Susan Czerski for continuing to offer your considerable talents to help me. Thank you to Teddy for your enthusiastic – and unfailingly loyal – company in all weathers. And thanks also to David Luxton, my incredibly talented literary agent.

To all of the players, coaches and leaders I have had the immense good fortune to work with and learn from, thank you. Experience is a great teacher and you have all given so freely.

I am very grateful to Jake. Thank you for sharing your drive, enthusiasm and ambition for the high performance message. And thank you for your friendship, support and encouragement too.

JAKE AND DAMIAN

We would both like to thank the *High Performance* team: Hannah Smith, Finn Ryan and Will O'Connor, thank you for sharing your skill, indefatigable spirit and unfailing humour. We are also grateful to the wider team at YMU – especially Alex McGuire, Holly Bott and Amanda Harris.

Thank you to all our podcast guests, for investing your trust in us and sharing your incredible wisdom, insights and lessons.

Thank you also to our brilliant editor, Rowan Borchers. Your guidance has been invaluable. Your faith, trust and support is appreciated. And thank you to the team at Penguin Random House for your passionate support of the initial idea and subsequent book.

Thank you to the authors and academics whose work ignited our interest in high performance and helped us to finesse our argument. The following books had a particular impact on us during our research, and offer a good starting point for anyone looking to learn more about high-performing people.

Viktor Frankl's *Man's Search for Meaning* offered some powerful insights that fed into the opening chapter on responsibility. Charles Duhigg's writing, particularly *Smarter Faster Better*, also informed our thinking on this subject, as well as providing useful material for the chapters on habits and culture. Jonathan Haidt's brilliant writing, particularly *The Happiness Hypothesis* and *The Coddling of the American Mind* (co-authored with Greg Lukianoff), were also sources of inspiration. Brad Stulberg and Steve Magness's *The Passion Paradox* proved a crucial book during our research on motivation, as did Daniel H. Pink's *Drive*, which provided several powerful case studies. Ceri Evans' work, and particularly his book *Perform Under Pressure,* provided an illuminating guide to the human brain and emotions. Our writing on emotions also draws upon Simon Marshall and Lesley Paterson's *The Brave Athlete*, as well as Steve Peters' ever-useful *The Chimp Paradox*.

Howard Gardner's work on multiple intelligences was a useful source for our writing on finding your strengths. Daniel Coyle's

The Talent Code was also important in shaping our thoughts about the origins of high performance. Carol Dweck's research into the growth mindset, particularly her book *Mindset*, was invaluable in the chapter on problem-solving. Chip and Dan Heath's *Switch* was profoundly useful for the chapter on consistency.

Jim Collins' writing on leadership is unfailingly wise: *Good to Great* was particularly useful. Willi Railo's writing on 'cultural architects' was another important source. Edgar Schein's whole back catalogue, especially *Humble Leadership* (co-written with his son Peter Schein) and *Organizational Culture and Leadership*, were critical in shaping the final two chapters. James Baron and Michael Hannan's work has also been invaluable.

Finally, thanks to you, the reader. We appreciate that, in an age of constant distraction, reading this book has involved a significant commitment of time and trust. We don't take this investment lightly. We hope *High Performance* has been as rewarding to read as it has been to write.

NOTES

Most of the quotations in this book come from our *High Performance* podcast interviews, transcripts and recordings of which can be found at www.thehighperformancepodcast. com. These notes include only quotations and case studies from elsewhere.

INTRODUCTION: NOTHING IS FIXED

1   Jim White. 'In this humble environment a group of future champion fighters is being nurtured'. *Telegraph*, 2 October 2004.

LESSON 1: TAKE RESPONSIBILITY

1   *Crawley and Horley Observer.* 'Horrific accident didn't stop Billy Monger from returning to the driver's seat', *Crawley and Horley Observer*, 25 January 2018. Available at: https://www. crawleyobserver.co.uk/sport/motorsport-horrific-accident-didnt-stop-billy-monger-returning-drivers-seat-2060613.
2   Albert Bandura. *Self-efficacy: The Exercise of Control.* New York, Freeman, 1997
3   For an overview of this theory, see Albert Bandura. 'Self-efficacy: toward a unifying theory of behavioural change.' *Psychological Review* 1977; 84(2): 191–215. This research is discussed in Charles Duhigg, *Smarter Faster Better*. London: Random House Business, 2016.
4   Alexandra Stocks, Kurt A April, Nandani Lynton. 'Locus of control and subjective well-being: a cross-cultural study'.

Problems and Perspectives in Management 2012; 10(1): 17–25. Cited in: Charles Duhigg. *Smarter Faster Better.*

5 Martin Seligman. 'Learned helplessness'. *Annual Review of Medicine* 1972; 23(1): 407–12. D Hiroto, Martin Seligman. 'Generality of learned helplessness in man'. *Journal of Personality and Social Psychology* 1977; 31(2): 311–27. Cited in: Martin Seligman. *Learned Optimism: How to Change Your Mind and Your Life.* New York: Vintage, 2006.

6 Clive White. 'Brain is not used by Van Persie'. *Telegraph*, 26 February 2005. Cited in: Andy Williams. *RVP: The Biography of Robin van Persie.* London: John Blake, 2013.

7 Rosamund Stone Zander and Benjamin Zander. *The Art of Possibility: Transforming Professional and Personal Life.* London: Penguin, 2002.

8 Sarah Butler. '"The support never stops" – former prisoner working for Timpson'. *Guardian*, 6 April 2019. Available at: https://www.theguardian.com/business/2019/apr/06/the-support-never-stops-says-prisoner-who-works-at-timpsons.

9 B L Walter, A G Shaikh in *Encyclopaedia of the Neurological Sciences* (2nd edn), 2014. J R Augustine. 'Chapter 9: The Reticular Formation'. In *Human Neuroanatomy* (2nd edn). Bognor Regis: John Wiley & Sons, 2006: 141–53.

10 R Hirt. 'Martin Seligman's journey from learned helplessness to learned happiness'. *Pennsylvania Gazette*, January/February 1999. Cited in: Martin Seligman. 'Building human strength: psychology's forgotten mission. *American Psychological Association Newsletter* 1998; 29(1). See also Seligman. *Learned Helplessness.*

11 Matt Rudd. 'The interview: Ant Middleton on Brexit, *SAS: Who Dares Wins* and manning up'. *The Times*, 14 April 2019. Available at: https://www.thetimes.co.uk/article/the-interview-nt-middleton-on-brexit-sas-who-dares-wins-and-manning-up-3c8knb0s0.

LESSON 2: GET MOTIVATED

1 Steven Gerrard. *My Story.* London: Penguin, 2016.
2 Ibid.

3   Ibid.

4   This story is recounted in: Dominic Fifield. 'This is a story of temptation – when Steven Gerrard almost joined Chelsea'. *The Athletic*, 11 May 2020. Available at: https://theathletic. com/1794799/2020/05/11/steven-gerrard-chelsea-liverpool-transfer-2005/; Steven Gerrard. *My Story*.

5   Steven Gerrard. *My Story*.

6   Jamie Carragher. '10: Steven Gerard'. *The Greatest Game* [podcast], 9 January 2020. Cited in: Dominic Fifield. 'This is a story of temptation'.

7   Rachel Hosie. 'How Zack George went from "massively overweight" child to the UK's fittest man, and how he trains to stay there'. *Insider*, 20 June 2020. Available at: https://www. insider.com/zack-george-became-uk-fittest-man-overweight-child-training-crossfit-2020-6.

8   Ibid.

9   The Deci and Ryan exercise described here features in a number of self-help books, most famously in Daniel H. Pink. *Drive: The Surprising Truth About What Motivates Us*. London: Canongate, 2011. For the original research see Richard Ryan, Edward Deci. 'Self-determination theory and the facilitation of intrinsic motivation, social development, and well-being'. *American Psychologist* 2000; 55(1): 68–78

10 Ibid.

11 Richard Ryan, Edward Deci. 'Self-determination theory'; Marylene Gagne, Edward Deci. 'Self-determination and work motivation'. *Journal of Organisational Behaviour* 2005; 26(4): 331–62; Patricia Chen, Phoebe C Ellsworth, Norbert Schwarz. 'Finding a fit or developing it: implicit theories about achieving passion for work'. *Personality and Social Psychology Bulletin* 2015; 41(10): 1411–24; Elle Luna. *The Crossroads of Should and Must*. New York: Workman, 2015; Dong Lui, Xiao-Ping Chen, Xin Yao. 'From autonomy to creativity: a multilevel investigation of the mediating role of harmonious passion'. *Journal of Applied Psychology* 2011; 96(2): 294–309.

12 Graham Jones and Adrian Moorhouse. *Developing Mental Toughness: Gold Medal Strategies for Transforming Your Business Performance.* London: Spring Hill Books, 2008.

13 Daniel H. Pink. *Drive.*

14 Sara James. 'Finding Your Passion: Work and the Authentic Self'. *M/C Journal*, 2015; 18(1). Cited in: Brad Stulberg, Steve Magness. *The Passion Paradox.* Emmaus, PA: Rodale, 2019.

15 Viktor E Frankl. *Man's Search for Meaning.* London: Simon & Schuster, 1997.

16 Lauren A Leotti, Sheena S Iyengar, Kevin N Ochsner. 'Born to choose: the origins and value of the need for control'. *Trends in Cognitive Sciences* 2010; 14(10): 457–63. Cited in: Charles Duhigg. *Smarter Faster Better.*

17 Mauricio R Delgado in Charles Duhigg, *Smarter Faster Better.*

18 VisionSport TV. 'Fan tells Redknapp: Scott Canham better than Lampard'. YouTube, 22 September 2014. Available at: https://www.youtube.com/watch?v=eAjd_jTvURc&t=0s. This story is also described in detail in: Oliver Kay. 'The Premier League 60: no 6, Frank Lampard'. *The Athletic*, 4 September 2020. Available at: https://theathletic.co.uk/2018585/2020/09/04/premier-league-60-frank-lampard/.

19 Frank Lampard. *Totally Frank: My Autobiography.* London: HarperCollins, 2006.

20 'Dylan Hartley retires from professional rugby'. Northampton Saints, 7 November 2019. Available at: https://www.northamptonsaints.co.uk/news/dylan-hartley-retires-from-professional-rugby.

21 Eddie Jones. *My Life and Rugby.* London: Macmillan, 2019.

22 Ibid.

LESSON 3: MANAGE YOUR EMOTIONS

1 Richard Moore. *Heroes, Villains and Velodromes: Chris Hoy and Britain's Track Cycling Revolution.* London: HarperSport, 2012.

2 Nick Townsend. 'Cycling: Hoy is ready to dig deep again and raid Olympic gold mine'. *Independent*, 23 October 2011.

Available at: https://www.independent.co.uk/sport/general/
others/cycling-hoy-is-ready-to-dig-deep-again-and-raid-
olympic-gold-mine-856512.html.

3   Simon Hattenstone. 'Kelly Holmes on mental health and happiness'. *Guardian*, 13 March 2019. Available at: https://www.
theguardian.com/sport/2019/mar/13/kelly-holmes-mental-
health-happiness-self-harming-podcast-interview.

4   Kelly Holmes. *Black, White & Gold: My Autobiography.*
London: Virgin Books, 2008.

5   Ibid.

6   Ant Middleton. *First Man In: Leading from the Front.* London:
HarperCollins, 2018.

7   Kelly Holmes. *Black, White & Gold.*

8   Ant Middleton. *First Man In.*

9   This description of the brain draws on Simon Marshall and
Lesley Paterson, *The Brave Athlete: Calm the F*ck Down and
Rise to the Occasion.* Boulder, CA: Velo Press, 2017.

10 Daniel H. Pink. *A Whole New Mind: Why Right-Brainers Will
Rule the Future.* New York: Riverhead Books, 2005.

11 James Watson. 'Foreword'. In: Sandra Ackerman. *Discovering
the Brain.* Washington, DC: National Academies Press, 1992.
Available at https://www.ncbi.nlm.nih.gov/books/NBK234155/.
Quoted in: Daniel H. Pink. *A Whole New Mind.*

12 Paul D MacLean. *The Triune Brain in Evolution: Role in
Paleocerebral Functions.* Cham: Springer, 1990.

13 Andrew Curran. *The Little Book of Big Stuff about the Brain:
The True Story of Your Amazing Brain.* Carmarthen: Crown
House Publishing, 2008.

14 Jonathan Haidt. *The Happiness Hypothesis: Putting Ancient
Wisdom to the Test of Modern Science.* London: Arrow,
2007.

15 'Optimising the performance of the human mind: Steve Peters at
TEDxYouth@Manchester 2012'. YouTube, 30 November 2012.
Available at: https://www.youtube.com/watch?v=R-KI1D5NPJs
&ab_channel=TEDxYouth.

16 Ibid.

17 For more information on this model, see Yehuda Shinar. *Think Like a Winner*. London: Vermilion, 2008.

18 For more information on this model, see Daniel Kahneman. *Thinking, Fast and Slow*. London: Penguin, 2012.

19 For more information on this model, see Steve Peters. *The Chimp Paradox: The Acclaimed Mind Management Programme to Help You Achieve Success, Confidence and Happiness*. London: Vermilion, 2012.

20 This model is outlined in: Ceri Evans. *Perform Under Pressure: Change the Way You Feel, Think and Act Under Pressure*. London: Thorsons, 2019.

21 Richard Lazarus. *Emotion and Adaptation* (paperback). Oxford: Oxford University Press, 1994. Also referenced in: Richard S Lazarus. 'Progress on a cognitive-motivational-relational theory of emotion'. *American Psychologist* 1991; 46(8): 819–34; Craig A Smith, Richard S Lazarus. 'Chapter 23: Emotion and adaptation'. In: Lawrence A Pervin (ed). *Handbook of Personality: Theory and Research*. New York, NY: Guilford, 1990: 609–37; S Folkman, R S Lazarus, R J Gruen, A DeLongis. 'Appraisal, health status and psychological symptoms'. *Journal of Personality and Social Psychology* 1986; 50(3): 571–79.

22 Richard Moore. *Heroes, Villains and Velodromes*.

23 Ibid.

24 Ibid.

25 This metaphor draws on an idea coined by Steven Covey, the 'emotional bank account'. See *The Seven Habits of Highly Successful People*. New York: Simon & Schuster, 1989.

LESSON 4: PLAY TO YOUR STRENGTHS

1 Tom Rath, Donald O Clifton. *How Full Is Your Bucket?* Washington, DC: Gallup Press, 2004. Also cited in: Donald O Clifton and Edward C Anderson. *StrengthsQuest: Discover and Develop Your Strengths in Academics, Career and Beyond*. Washington, DC: Gallup Press, 2002.

2   Roy F Baumeister, Ellen Bratslavsky, Catrin Finkenauer, Kathleen D Vohs. 'Bad is stronger than good'. *Review of General Psychology* 2001; 5(4) 323–70.

3   Howard Gardner. *Frames of Mind: The Theory of Multiple Intelligences*. New York, NY: Basic Books, 2011.

4   *Belfast Telegraph*. 'Scents and sensibility: we chat to perfume maker Jo Malone'. *Belfast Telegraph*, 20 February 2016. Available at: https://www.belfasttelegraph.co.uk/life/features/scents-and-sensibility-we-chat-to-perfume-maker-jo-malone-34457693.html.

5   Rebecca Gonsalves. 'Jo Malone interview: how one of the greatest names in perfumery discovered life after cancer'. *Independent*, 12 February 2015. Available at: https://www.independent.co.uk/life-style/fashion/features/jo-malone-interview-how-one-greatest-names-perfumery-discovered-life-after-cancer-a6866426.html.

6   Zoe Forsey. 'I was kicked out of school at 17 – but at 26 my company employs 700 people. *Mirror*, 22 August 2019. Available at: https://www.mirror.co.uk/tv/tv-news/kicked-out-school-17–26-18963997.

7   Ibid.

8   Charles Handy. *The Second Curve*. London: Random House Business Books, 2015.

9   Kelly Holmes. *Black, White & Gold*.

10 Robert B Cialdini. *Influence: The Psychology of Persuasion*. London: HarperBusiness, 2007. Also cited in: Noah J Goldstein, Steve J Martin, Robert B Cialdini. *Yes! 50 Secrets from the Science of Persuasion*. London: Profile Books, 2007.

11 Kruger and Dunning's is cited in a number of popular psychology books. For one recent example, see Aaron Claarey. *The Curse of the High IQ*. Create Space, 2016. For the original research, see Justin Kruger, David Dunning. 'Unskilled and unaware of it: how difficulties in recognizing one's own incompetence lead to inflated self-assessments'. *Journal of Personality and Social Psychology* 1999; 77(6): 1121–34.

12 Brian Resnick. 'Intellectual humility: the importance of knowing you might be wrong,' *Vox*, 4 January 2019. Available at: https://www.vox.com/science-and-health/2019/1/4/17989224/intellectual-humility-explained-psychology-replication. Also cited in: Adam Grant. *Think Again*. London: Random House, 2021.

13 Kelly Holmes. *Black, White & Gold*.

14 Mihaly Csikszentmihalyi. *Flow: The Psychology of Happiness*. London: Ebury, 2013. Also see Csikszentmihalyi's TED Talk, 'Flow: The secret to happiness'. TED, February 2004. Available at: https://www.ted.com/talks/mihaly_csikszentmihalyi_flow_the_secret_to_happiness?language=en. This account of flow also draws on Daniel H. Pink, *Drive*.

15 Kelly Holmes. *Black, White & Gold*.

LESSON 5: GET FLEXIBLE

1 Amos Tversky, Daniel Kahneman. 'Judgment under uncertainty: heuristics and biases'. *Science* 1974; 185(4157): 1124–31.

2 Donald McRae. 'Ben Ainslie: "The ultimate goal is to bring the America's Cup back to Britain"'. *Guardian*, 22 May 2017. Available at: https://www.theguardian.com/sport/2017/may/22/ben-ainslie-americas-cup-britain-bermuda.

3 Rory Carroll. 'America's Cup: Sir Ben Ainslie's Oracle Team USA clinches stunning comeback'. *Guardian*, 26 September 2013. Available at: https://www.theguardian.com/sport/2013/sep/25/americas-cup-victory-team-usa-comeback.

4 Ibid.

5 BBC Sport. 'How did Sir Ben Ainslie help inspire America's Cup win?' *BBC Sport*, 26 September 2013. Available at: https://www.bbc.co.uk/sport/sailing/24285864.

6 Chris Maxwell. 'Sir Ben Ainslie on business and his bid to win Britain's first America's cup'. *Director*, 15 July 2016. Available at: https://www.director.co.uk/sir-ben-ainslie-land-rover-bar-18821-2/.

7   *Country & Town House.* 'Interview: Ben Ainslie, the Trophy Hunter'. *Country & Town House*, July 2016. Available at: https:// www.countryandtownhouse.co.uk/culture/sir-ben-ainslie-americas-cup/.

8   Carol Dweck. *Mindset: How You Can Fulfil Your Potential.* London: Robinson, 2012. This account of Dweck's research also draws on Matthew Syed, *Bounce: The Myth of Talent and the Power of Practice.* London: Fourth Estate, 2011; and Chip and Dan Heath, *Switch: How to Change When Change Is Hard.* London: Random House Business Books, 2011.

9   Carol Dweck. *Mindset.*

10 Carol Dweck. 'The power of believing you can improve'. TEDxNorrkoping, 1 November 2014. Available at: https:// www.ted.com/talks/carol_dweck_the_power_of_believing_ that_you_can_improve.

11 The 'candle problem' is described in a number of works on popular psychology, including Daniel Pink's TED Talk: 'The puzzle of motivation'. TEDGlobal, 2009. Available at: https://www.ted. com/talks/dan_pink_the_puzzle_of_motivation?language=en. For the original research see Karl Dunker. 'On problem-solving'. *Psychological Monographs* 1945; 58(5): 1–113.

12 Puzzles like these are widely used in training workshops and are frequently cited in popular psychology books. For these examples, I drew on Shane Snow, *Dream Teams: Working Together Without Falling Apart.* New York: Portfolio, 2018.

13 Simon Kuper, Stefan Szymanski. *Soccernomics: Why England Loses, Why Spain, Germany, and Brazil Win, and Why the US, Japan, Australia Lose.* London: Nation Books, 2014.

14 Eleanor Lawrie. 'Not on the High Street's Holly Tucker: "Grey-haired investors laughed at us when we asked for funding – to them we were just two women who sold crafts"'. *This Is Money*, 14 March 2015. Available at: https://www.thisismoney. co.uk/money/smallbusiness/article-3485732/Not-High-Street-s-Holly-Tucker-investors-just-women-sold-crafts.html. See also

Sophie Cornish and Holly Tucker. *Build a Business From Your Kitchen Table: The Business Plan*. London: Simon & Schuster, 2014.

15 Alison Reynolds, David Lewis. 'Teams solve problems faster when they're more cognitively diverse'. *Harvard Business Review*, 30 March 2017. Available at: https://hbr.org/2017/03/teams-solve-problems-faster-when-theyre-more-cognitively-diverse.

16 Eleanor Lawrie. 'Not on the High Street's Holly Tucker: "Grey-haired investors laughed at us when we asked for funding – to them we were just two women who sold crafts"'.

LESSON 6: FIND YOUR NON-NEGOTIABLES

1 Paul Doyle. 'All hail Sir Clive Woodward'. *Guardian*, 1 November 2005. Available at: https://www.theguardian.com/football/2005/nov/01/sport.comment.

2 Clive Woodward. *How to Win*. London: Hodder & Stoughton, 2019. For a longer version of this story, see Clive Woodward. *Winning! The Path to Rugby World Cup Glory*. London: Hodder, 2005.

3 Ibid.

4 Roy Keane. *Keane: The Autobiography*. London: Penguin, 2011.

5 Michael Beer, Russell A Eisenstat, Bert Spector. *The Critical Path to Corporate Renewal*. Boston, MA: Harvard Business School Press, 1990. Cited in: Chip and Dan Heath. *Switch*.

6 Clive Woodward. *How to Win*.

7 Dave Woods. 'Shaun Wane: How Wigan teenage tearaway turned his life around to become rugby league royalty'. *BBC Sport*, 14 May 2019. Available at: https://www.bbc.co.uk/sport/rugby-league/48258034.

8 Charles Duhigg. *The Power of Habit: Why We Do What We Do, and How to Change*. London: Penguin, 2013.

9 This account of Peter Gollwitzer's research draws on Chip and Dan Heath's *Switch*. For the original research, see Peter M Gollwitzer, Sarah Milne, Paschal Sheeran, Thomas L Webb. 'Implementation intentions and health behaviours'. In: Mark

Conner, Paul Norman (eds.), *Predicting Health Behaviour: Research and Practice with Social Cognition Models* (2nd edn). Buckingham: Open University Press, 2005.

10 James Clear. *Atomic Habits*. London: Random House Business Books, 2018.

11 John Wooden, Steve Jamison. *The Wisdom of Wooden: My Century On and Off the Court*. New York, NY: McGraw-Hill Contemporary, 2010. Cited in: Robert Maurer. *One Small Step Can Change Your Life: The Kaizen Way*. New York, NY: Workman, 2004.

12 James Clear. *Atomic Habits*.

13 James March. *A Primer on Decision Making: How Decisions Happen*. London: Simon & Schuster, 1994.

14 Chip and Dan Heath. *Switch*.

15 James Clear. 'Avoid the second mistake'. JamesClear.com. Available at: https://jamesclear.com/second-mistake. See also James Clear. *Atomic Habits*.

LESSON 7: LEAD THE TEAM

1   George Flood. 'South Africa captain Siya Kolisi after Rugby World Cup win: "We can achieve anything if we work together as one"'. *Evening Standard*, 2 November 2019. Available at: https://www.standard.co.uk/sport/rugby/south-africa-captain-siya-kolisi-after-rugby-world-cup-win-we-can-achieve-anything-if-we-work-together-as-one-a4276971.html.

2   'Siya Kolisi: "We represent something much bigger"'. *Guardian*, 6 June 2018. Available at: https://www.theguardian.com/sport/2018/jun/06/siya-kolisi-interview-south-africa-first-black-test-captain-england.

3   David Walsh. 'The Interview: Siya Kolisi, South Africa's World Cup winning rugby captain, on escaping poverty and hunger'. *Sunday Times*, 19 January 2020. Available at: https://www.thetimes.co.uk/article/the-interview-siya-kolisi-south-africas-world-cup-winning-rugby-captain-on-escaping-poverty-and-hunger-j7trtnb08.

4   Floyd Henry Allport. 'The influence of the group upon asso-
    ciation and thought'. *Journal of Experimental Psychology*
    1920; 3(3): 159–82. Also cited in: G P Brooks, R W Johnson.
    'Floyd Allport and the master problem of social psych-
    ology'. *Psychological Report* 1978; 42(1): 295–308.

5   Satyan Mukherjee et, al., 'Prior shared success predicts victory in
    team competitions'. *Nature Human Behaviour*, 2019; 3(74–81).

6   Reid Hoffman. *The Start-Up of You: Adapt to the Future,
    Invest in Yourself, and Transform Your Career.* New York, NY:
    Currency, 2012.

7   James C Collins, Jerry I Porras. *Built to Last: Successful Habits
    of Visionary Companies.* New York, NY: HarperCollins, 1994.

8   Chip and Dan Heath. *Switch.*

9   Andy Jones. 'Sean Dyche exclusive: the managers who
    shaped me'. *The Athletic*, 11 May 2020. Available at: https://
    theathletic.co.uk/1802950/2020/05/11/sean-dyche-burnley-
    watford-chesterfield/. This account of Sean Dyche's impact on
    Burnley FC also draws on Dave Thomas, *Champions: The Story
    of Burnley's Instant Return to the Premier League.* Worthing:
    Pitch Publishing, 2016.

10 Ibid.

11 Andy Jones. 'Seven years of Dyche: dressing room dancing,
    "Gaffer's Day" and showing he cares (just don't play him at
    golf)'. *The Athletic*, 30 October 2019. Available at: https://
    theathletic.co.uk/1333098/2019/10/30/seven-years-of-dyche-
    dressing-room-dancing-gaffers-day-and-showing-he-cares-
    just-dont-play-him-at-golf/.

12 Ibid.

13 Chip and Dan Heath. *Switch.*

14 Jim Collins. *Good to Great.* London: Random House Business
    Books, 2001. See also Jim Collins. 'Best New Year's Resolution?
    A "stop doing" list'. 30 December 2003. Available at: https://
    www.jimcollins.com/article_topics/articles/best-new-years.
    html.

15 Peter Bregman. *18 Minutes: Find Your Focus, Master Distraction
    and Get the Right Things Done.* London: Orion, 2012.

16 Ben Machell. 'How Ben Francis built the billion-pound fitness brand Gymshark'. *The Times*, 5 December 2020. Available at: https://www.thetimes.co.uk/article/how-ben-francis-built-the-billion-pound-fitness-brand-gymshark-crls00h2n.

17 Ben Francis. 'Why I stepped down as Gymshark CEO'. *Ben Francis*, 11 May 2020. Available at: https://www.benfrancis.com/article/why-i-stepped-down-as-gymshark-ceo/.

18 Jon Robinson. 'Gymshark founder reveals reasons behind stepping down as CEO'. *Insider*, 14 May 2020. Available at: https://www.insidermedia.com/news/midlands/gymshark-founder-reveals-reasons-behind-stepping-down-as-ceo.

19 Ben Francis. 'Why I stepped down as Gymshark CEO'.

20 Solomon E Asch. 'Opinions and social pressure'. *Scientific American* 1955; 193(5): 31–35. Also cited in: Harold Guetzkow. *Groups, Leadership and Men*. Lancaster: Carnegie Press, 1951; Vernon Allen, John Levine. 'Social support and conformity: the role of independent assessment of reality'. *Journal of Experimental Social Psychology* 1971; 7(1): 48–58.

21 Solomon E Asch. 'Opinions and social pressure'.

22 For Railo quote, see Sven-Göran Eriksson, Willi Railo. *Sven-Göran Eriksson On Management* (new edn). London: Carlton Books, 2002. Also cited in: Line D Danielsen, Rune Giske, Derek M Peters, Rune Høigaard. 'Athletes as "cultural architects": a qualitative analysis of elite coaches' perceptions of highly influential soccer players'. *The Sport Psychologist* 2019; 33(4): 313–22. For Solskjær quote, see 'Solskjaer considering Manchester United captain contenders. *Manchester Evening News*, 13 April 2019. Available at: https://www.manchestereveningnews.co.uk/sport/football/football-news/manchester-united-news-now-today-16119832.

LESSON 8: CRAFT A CULTURE

1 Guillem Balagué. *Brave New World: Inside Pochettino's Spurs*. London: Orion, 2019.

2   Ibid.

3   David Hytner. 'Energía universal: how Pochettino has driven the Tottenham revolution'. *Guardian*, 29 April 2017. Available at: https://www.theguardian.com/football/blog/2017/apr/29/energia-universal-mauricio-pochetinno-tottenham-revolution.

4   Rhiannon Beaubien, Shane Parrish. *The Great Mental Models Volume 1: General Thinking Concepts.* Ottawa: ON: Latticework, 2020.

5   This account of Baron and Hannan's research draws on: Charles Duhigg. *Smarter Faster Better: The Secrets of Being Productive in Life and Business.* London: Random House, 2016.

6   James N Baron, Michael T Hannan. 'The economic sociology of organisational entrepreneurship: lessons from the Stanford Project on emerging companies'. In: Victor Nee, Richard Swedberg (eds). *The Economic Sociology of Capitalism.* New York, NY: Russell Sage, 2002: 168–203. Quoted in: Charles Duhigg. *Smarter Faster Better.*

7   Sid Lowe. *Fear and Loathing in La Liga: Barcelona vs Real Madrid.* London: Vintage, 2014.

8   Charles Duhigg. *Smarter Faster Better.*

9   James N Baron, Michael T Hannan. 'Organisational Blueprints for Success'; James N Baron, M Diane Burton, Michael T Hannan. 'The road taken: origins and evolution of employment systems in emerging companies'. *Industrial and Corporate Change* 1996; 5(2): 239–. Both quoted in: Charles Duhigg. *Smarter Faster Better.*

10 Paul J Zak. *Trust Factor: The Science of Creating High-Performance Companies.* New York, NY: AMACOM, 2017.

11 Thanks to Bill Beswick for this anecdote. Beswick recounts a similar story in 'Great minds think alike'. BBC News, 13 August 2001. Available at: http://news.bbc.co.uk/sport1/hi/football/eng_prem/1484852.stm.

12 Jim Collins. *Good to Great.*

13 Adam M Grant, Elizabeth M Campbell, Grace Chen, Keenan Cotttone, David Lapedis, Karen Lee. 'Impact and the art of

motivation maintenance: the effects of contact with beneficiaries on persistence behaviour'. *Organizational Behavior and Human Decision Processes* 2007; 103(1): 53–67. Cited in: Adam Grant. *Give and Take: Why Helping Others Drives Our Success.* London: W&N, 2014.

14 The Netball Show. '52: Netball Show: Tracey Neville Retirement'. *The Netball Show* [podcast].

15 Matt Dickinson. 'Tracey Neville interview: "I've the calmer, maybe softer side but like Gary I have that impatience"'. *The Times*, 19 April 2018. Available at: https://www.thetimes. co.uk/article/tracey-neville-interview-ive-the-calmer-maybe-softer-side-but-like-gary-i-have-that-impatience-vjwh3j287.

16 Oliver Brown. 'Tracey Neville interview: "Usually people ask me about my brothers Gary and Philip – to have the roles reversed makes me break down"'. *Telegraph*, 22 May 2018. Available at: https://www.telegraph.co.uk/netball/2018/05/22/tracey-neville-interview-usually-people-ask-brothers-gary-phillip/

17 Ibid.

18 Taiichi Ohno. *Toyota Production System: Beyond Large-Scale Production.* New York, NY: Productivity Press, 1988.

19 Fred Rees, Duncan Humphreys (dirs). *Living With The Lions.* Ocelot Films, 1999.

20 This exploration of emotional intelligence draws on: Anita Williams Woolley, Christopher F Chabris, Alex Pentland, Nada Hashmi, Thomas W Malone, Anita Williams Wooley. 'Evidence for a collective intelligence factor in the performance of human groups'. *Science* 2010; 330(6004): 686–88. Cited in: Charles Duhigg. *Smarter Faster Better.*

21 S Baron-Cohen, T Jolliffe, C Mortimore, M Robertson. 'Another advanced test of theory of mind: evidence from very high functioning adults with autism or Asperger syndrome'. *Journal of Child Psychology and Psychiatry* 1997; 38(7): 813–22; S Baron-Cohen, S Wheelwright, J Hill, Y Raste, I Plumb. 'The "Reading the Minds in the Eyes" Test Revised Version: a study with normal adults, and adults with Asperger syndrome or high-functioning autism'. *Journal of Child Psychology*

and Psychiatry 2001; 42(2): 241–51. Both quoted in: Charles Duhigg. *Smarter Faster Better.*

22 Travis Bradberry, Jean Greaves. *Emotional Intelligence 2.0.* San Diego, CA: TalentSmart, 2009.

23 Raj Bains. 'Kevin Sinfield: the low-key legend'. *Vice*, 17 December 2025. Available at: https://www.vice.com/en/article/ 4xjggn/kevin-sinfield-the-low-key-legend.

24 Gareth Ellis, conversation with the author.

25 Jason Booth, conversation with the author.

26 This exploration of psychological safety draws on: Amy C Edmondson. *The Fearless Organization: Creating Psychological Safety in the Workplace for Learning, Innovation, and Growth.* Hoboken, NJ: John Wiley & Sons, 2018. Quoted in: Charles Duhigg. *Smarter Faster Better.* Also referenced in: Amy C Edmondson. *A Fuller Explanation: The Synergetic Geometry of R Buckminster Fuller.* New York, NY: Van Nostrand Reinhold, 1992; Bertrand Moingeon, Amy Edmondson. *Organizational Learning and Competitive Advantage.* London: SAGE Publications, 1996.

27 Charles Duhigg. *Smarter Faster Better.*

28 Charles Duhigg. 'What Google learned from its quest to build the perfect team'. *New York Times*, 25 February 2016. Available at: https://www.nytimes.com/2016/02/28/magazine/what-google-learned-from-its-quest-to-build-the-perfect-team.html.

29 Amy Edmondson. 'Extreme teaming in an uncertain world'. *Life Science Leader*, 6 April 2018. Available at: https://www. lifescienceleader.com/doc/extreme-teaming-in-an-uncertain-world-0001. Quoted in: Charles Duhigg. *Smarter Faster Better.*

30 Amy C Edmondson. *The Fearless Organization*; Amy C Edmondson, Jean-François Harvey. *Extreme Teaming: Lessons in Complex, Cross-Sector Leadership.* Bingley: Emerald Group Publishing, 2017. Quoted in: Charles Duhigg. *Smarter Faster Better.*

31 Adam Bryant. 'Google's quest to build a better boss'. *New York Times*, 12 March 2011. Available at https://www.nytimes. com/2011/03/13/business/13hire.html.

32 Emily Croydon, Katie Falkingham. 'Tracey Neville and Ama Agbeze: England pair talk captain-coach dynamics'. *BBC Sport*, 11 October 2018. Available at: https://www.bbc.co.uk/sport/netball/45827561.

33 Amy C Edmondson. *The Fearless Organization*. London: Wiley, 2018.

34 Michiel de Hoog. '6 secret traits that make Louis van Gaal the humble genius he is (and mainstream media fail to see)'. *De Correspondent*, 8 August 2014. Available at: https://thecorrespondent.com/1418/6-secret-traits-that-make-louis-van-gaal-the-humble-genius-he-is-and-mainstream-media-fail-to-see/125220977970-aab230c0.

INDEX